I LOVE YOU I HATE YOU

CARLOS G. VALLES

I I
LOVE HATE
YOU YOU

Triumph™ Books
Tarrytown, New York

Library of Congress Cataloging-in-Publication Data
Vālesa, Father, 1925–
    I love you, I hate you / Carlos G. Valles. — 1st ed.
        p.   cm.
    ISBN 0-8007-3036-4
    1. Interpersonal relations.   2. Love-hate relationships.
I. Title.
HM132.V35   1992
158′.2—dc20   91-38168
                                                    CIP

Copyright © 1992 by Carlos G. Valles
Published by Triumph™ Books
Tarrytown, New York
An Imprint of Gleneida Publishing Group
Printed in the United States of America
First Edition

A woman told a man:
—I love you.
The man answered:
—My heart deserves your love.
The woman said:
—Perchance you do not love me?
And the man looked up to her and kept silent.
Then the woman shouted:
—I hate you!
And the man said:
—In that case, my heart also deserves your hatred.

Kahlil Gibran

Contents

Mommy Is Stupid!

Psychologists speak of love-hate relationships. The human heart is deeper than any human can understand, and the most unlikely mixtures take place in it with astounding ease. Even opposite extremes can be reconciled there in cheerful coexistence, much to the bewilderment of the heart's owner, who can be shocked to see how he or she can suddenly feel despondent in the midst of elation, resentful while grateful, and viciously destructive while tenderly loving. The most sacred feelings can go hand in hand with the meanest inclinations, and hell can mix with heaven in the throbbing mystery that the human heart is.

The point of this book is to suggest that every human relationship is, to a greater or lesser degree, a love-hate relationship, and that to grasp and accept this fact and act accordingly is an important way to improve those relationships, and with them the affective tone of our lives. We are what we are, we enjoy and suffer what we suffer and enjoy, largely because of the way we

relate to those persons, far and near, whom we meet daily, talk
with, think about, love and cherish, fear and resent. Our relationships shape our lives, and if we, in turn, learn how to shape
our relationships, we shall be taking a long step toward a happier
life and a more useful existence.

Mixtures are always tricky to analyze. We find it easier to
handle all-or-nothing, black-or-white, saint-or-sinner, hero-or-
villain situations, and to divide people into friends and foes, or
simply people we like and people we dislike, with a no-man's-
land of indifferent characters in between. But the reality is a little
more complex and challenging. The fact is that even our best
friend can become momentarily a foe, and even in the purest
love there can be a streak of hatred, disturbingly real in its irra-
tional presence.

Our first reaction when faced with this unpleasant discovery is
to deny the reality, to ignore the shadow, to disguise the unworthy feeling. How can I hate my friend whom I love with all my
heart? This was just a passing cloud of uncertain origin, quickly
to be dismissed from our attention before it can mar the beauty
of the intimate relationship. The trouble is that by dismissing the
thought, we endanger the friendship; by hiding the seed of dis-
cord, we foster its growth; by refusing to look into our heart with
impartial honesty, we miss the chance of feeling its beat and
healing its wounds. The negative feeling was implanted right in
the middle of the positive regard, and it is there that we have to
examine it for the better integration of our complex selves. Acceptance of the mixture is the first condition toward understanding it.

The mixture was in us almost from the beginning of our conscious lives, and it was first freely expressed with the naive innocence of the guileless child. It was only later, as we grew and we
learned what is proper and can be expressed, and what is im-

proper and has to be carefully hidden from society by the polite dissembling we call good manners, that we first repressed from expression, and then withdrew from consciousness, the explicit admission of out-of-place feelings. Here is an example of my own experience, which clearly brings to light the existence of such contradictory feelings at the same time in a normal child, and also points out gently the source of the contradiction. We all can readily recognize ourselves in that dear child.

In a family I know well, I was once greeted with the joyful news of the latest event at home. The small child, who for some time already was babbling more or less intelligible sounds, had that day pronounced clearly and distinctly her first grammatically complete sentence. It was a sentence with subject, verb, and predicate, all in correct order and with perfect meaning, which qualified the growing candidate for a place in talking mankind, first step in a linguistic career that would last a lifetime of words without end. The family had been quick to react at the early prowess of its smaller member, the neighbors had been duly informed, phone calls had been made, and I, lucky to enter the house during the auspicious flurry, was at once informed with explosive delight of the latest feat of the scholarly child. It was almost a home graduation ceremony.

With all the fuss of the occasion, they almost forgot to tell me what the child had actually said. The sentence itself seemed unimportant, compared to the momentous fact of its having been pronounced. But the sentence was significant, very significant indeed, and gave a quick but valuable glimpse into the mentality of that child who had just joined the literate world. The small girl had declared with clear and definite pronunciation: "Mommy is stupid."

There it was. Famous first words. Opening sentence in the eventful autobiography of a child who finds speech. Window to

a character. Headline for a family report. "Mommy is stupid."
They all commented with glee on the striking words. "Isn't she
clever?" "What a cute child!" "Say it again that we all may hear
it." Meanwhile the child stood in the center, acknowledging the
flood of compliments, and looking a little surprised that such an
obvious and simple statement should have caused such surprise
and admiration among the bystanders. Was it not evident to all
around that her mother was stupid?

We understand the sequence of events that has led up to that
bold conclusion in the child's mind. The little girl surely loves
her mother, she has clung to her from the very first moment of
her existence, she has experienced her closeness, her care, her
tenderness, in the daily dependence for every need and every
caress with unfailing devotion. She knows that she is everything
to her mother, and she has only to hit a high note on her crying
scale for her mother to run to her side, take her in her arms, and
press her to her heart.

Or rather, that is how things were for some time at the beginning; her mother was always close at hand, and the little girl had
absolute priority over any other person or event that might attempt to claim her mother's attention. But now of late things
seem to be changing at home, the little girl is surprised and hurt
at the change, and wants to set things right before it is too late.
Now her mother leaves her alone for long periods and disappears
without notice into the kitchen or out to the garden, and there is
no telling when she will come back. The unfailing resource of
the high-pitched cry does not seem to work anymore, as the most
mother does is come in for a moment, say a few words, and
disappear again hurriedly into her absurd errands. "Does she not
understand that I am the most important thing she has to care
about? Does she not realize that no work in the kitchen or in the
garden can justify her leaving me alone like this when I need her

and call her? And if she does not realize this, is she not stupid by any standard you may judge? That is what she is, and that is what I will proclaim before the world once I find speech and get an audience. Yes, Mommy is stupid."

There, in the candid words of an innocent child, is the first expression and clear picture of a love-hate relationship. There is love in the little girl for her mother, and she would not speak with that freedom and spontaneity if she were not sure in her heart that her words will not alienate her mother from her, but will bring her closer. But then there is also resentment, remonstration, complaint. There is a sharp urge of rebellion and protest at the incomprehensible and untenable behavior of the mother. There is the frightening will to hurt a beloved being by publicly using in open attack the word that in the child's incipient vocabulary denotes the greatest offense, condemnation, and rejection: *stupid*. The girl has made family history by the intensity of her feelings and the clarity of her expression. And the ambivalent feeling toward her mother, as in due time it will be about everybody else around, has taken firm root in the tender heart. The time for pure, unmixed feelings, if there ever was any, is already over, and life has begun to be for her, as it is for each one of us, the puzzling mixture that keeps forever surprising and challenging us from within our very selves.

If the little girl had found this double feeling within herself, it is not less true that she had silently learned it also from her mother. Her mother also has a similar ambivalent feeling toward her, though neither mother nor daughter may be explicitly aware of it, and the mother's feeling has cast its imprint on the daughter's heart in the daily anonymous teaching of the family school. The mother loves her daughter more than anything else on earth, looks after her in every minor detail and constant care with total dedication and infinite tenderness, would willingly and readily give her own life to save her daughter if this were necessary.

All this is true, and there are no words in any language adequate to describe the depth and intensity and generosity of a mother's love toward her newborn child. And yet, together with all this, it is equally and importantly true that the mother harbors a deep, persistent, dark resentment against her own child. The child has brought her happiness, fulfillment, motherhood; but the child has also taken much away from her: freedom to move, independence to act, freshness of body, and lightness of mind. The mother now has first to think of the child when she plans or wants or thinks of anything. A cry at an unearthly hour may ruin a night's sleep, and an untimely fever may mean the last-minute cancellation of a well-planned trip. Although the mother will cancel the trip and get up at night with the spontaneous response of her motherly instinct, there is a hidden cloud of disturbing annoyance that will unknowingly darken the recesses of her soul. Sacrifices are recorded and vigils are counted in the archives of the mind. The protest mounts and the rebellion brews. The mother's attitude toward her child is from its very inception a love-hate relationship, and the child senses it, mirrors it, grasps it, and reacts to his or her mother with the same compound feeling he or she reads in the mother. The first school of love, in the home, is a school of mixed feelings. The curriculum is set for life.

Once I witnessed an explicit enactment of this instructive situation. This was not the mother, but the father of the child, in this case another little girl of only a few months. The father's masculine impatience sharpened the reaction, but that only made visible what in a more hidden way was taking place in the mother's subconscious. The man arrived home from his work in the evening, and the first thing he did in the eagerness of his affection was to look for the child and make straight for the cradle where she was sleeping. He took the little girl in his arms, not with the studied care to let her sleep, but with sudden jerks to make sure that she woke up and stayed awake. I was surprised at his behavior and asked him, "Why do you do that?" He answered at once with defenseless sincerity: "If she sleeps now, she won't sleep at night and won't let me sleep. And I need my sleep. So let her wake up now, and then we'll all have our sleep together at night." Honest man that he was. The blessedness of being a father did not take away the misery of being a nonprofessional baby-sitter.

Before I proceed, I mention a practical conclusion I have drawn for myself from such repeated cases. I avoid having to wake up anybody from sleep; I escape, find excuses, or simply refuse to oblige if someone asks me to wake him or her up at a fixed time. They ask it as a favor, and will be grateful if I comply and shake them into wakefulness at the time they have determined. Or so they say. That is, they will thank me outwardly and sincerely for having done that for them, but inwardly in their heart of hearts, as indeed in their whole shaken body, they will resent my interference and curse my intervention, as their whole shaken body will show. Their mind will express gratitude, but their sleepy eyes will proclaim their protest at my thoughtless aggression, and their yawning mouth, their slowed-down brain, and their uncertain step will join in the protest. We all harbor a resentment against the person who wakes us up, even if we had asked him or her to do so. And I want to avoid, as far as possible, collecting negative points from people I have to deal with. Let others put up with the odium of cutting short a person's lawful sleep.

It is usually the parents who have to wake up their children daily in the early morning to get ready in time for school. They do that for their good, to be sure, though some children would sincerely doubt what good going to school does them; but still the body resents what the mind accepts, and every morning reveille is a covert oppression, and the inward protest for it is directed toward the loving parent who suffers as much as the child in the morning chill. To wake up people, I firmly believe, is the job of alarm clocks. That is why they were invented. And let the machine take the rap.

The girl is not allowed to sleep when she wants. Soon she will not be allowed to eat what she wants or when she wants or where she wants. She will not be allowed to do what she wants, to go where she wants. She will not be allowed to play with dirt, to cross the street, to eat sweets, to puddle in the rain. Prohibitions will pile up all around her without her understanding what all the fuss is about. Why should she have to eat at fixed times, and only certain foods, and only measured amounts? Why should she have to put on socks and wash her hands and comb her hair? Her parents explain that all this is for her own good, but that is too abstract a thought to be entertained in her straightforward mind. The fact is that she is deprived of many wishes, and made to do things she definitely dislikes, and that it is her parents who are responsible for such unpleasant orders. These distasteful experiences mar unavoidably the interaction between parents and children in the best of homes. To ignore this situation is to endanger all future relationships in the family.

In another home, Daddy and Mommy were discussing their child. I was present, and so was the child, a three-year-old girl who was playing with seeming detachment in a corner of the room while our talk was going on. The talk was on an important decision to be made soon: to which kindergarten to send the girl, since good institutions are hard to find, and a place had to be reserved early. While the parents spoke, I looked at the child. What was she thinking? What was she understanding? Children may be small, but they have ears and a brain and a sharp sense that warns them of danger before new and threatening situations.

And here was one such. Daddy and Mommy were talking about sending her somewhere, and for long periods of time and in someone else's care. What could all that mean? What dark plot was being hatched to get rid of her? Were all her suspicions about family dealings to come true finally? The girl remained silent through the discussion, and at the end, when we got up, she faced her parents and said with an uncertain voice, "Are you going to give me away?" A deep wound in a tender soul.

It is clear that the cause of such negative feelings in the family is not any wrong or faulty behavior, and that nobody is to blame and nobody should feel guilty about doing necessary things that unavoidably strain relationships at home. The parents have to send the child to school, and the child is fully entitled to manifest his or her likes and dislikes and fight for them while finding out the complexities of human life. The dark side of the love-hate relationship is not necessarily, and not usually, due to bad behavior on the part of those who make up the relationship. It is important to realize this in order to clear the air and lighten the mind while discussing this complex situation. The word *hate* is so strong that one hesitates to use it, for oneself or for others, in the sacred context of family relationships. Let it be clear, then, that here there is question of a spontaneous negative feeling which arises through no one's fault in the course of the normal life of the family. There is no moral condemnation attached to it, and this should make it easy for us to recognize it, own it, and express it. The tendency to hide it from ourselves and from others is precisely what makes it particularly dangerous. To face the problem is to solve it.

Now a mother's testimony, again in the informal setting of a casual visit. She had come to see me with an invitation to a function, and had brought along her young son, not to leave him alone at home. I asked with a smile, in an attempt to ingratiate myself to the youngster, who did not seem particularly happy at seeing me, "And what is this young man's name?" Before he could open his mouth, his mother answered for him with quick indictment: "His name is . . . Satan! You have only to see the way he behaves." I was shocked; the boy began to cry, and his mother, instantly changed from hatred to love, took him to herself, pressed him against her breast, started caressing him, kissing him, and repeating in the most loving tone, "No, no, you are my child, you are a good boy, and your mother loves you very, very much and never will say such a thing again."

Quite a scene. The change of stage had been so sudden that it seemed almost impossible that the same person should have played opposite roles in such a swift transformation. Anger and affection, spite and tenderness, insult and praise. She made up profusely for the unwary word. The boy fell silent and wiped his tears. But he would not easily forget the unfair affront before an outside witness. And the cruel blow would in turn strike sparks of rebellion within his own heart. Someday he will find himself addressing his mother in thoughtless words whose origin he himself will wonder about, only to repent at once and assure her of his love and devotion for life. Both will be bewildered at the unexpected outburst, as they were bewildered in their flaring confrontation before me. If they had learned to know their own hearts and plumb their misleading depths already from that early experience and others that undoubtedly took place in early days, they would have found it easier to cope with the same situation as it appeared again and again throughout their lifelong relationship. Thus they might have minimized its recurrence and healed its wounds. The earlier we learn, the better.

The Camel Driver's Turban

The understanding of the love-hate relationship, once stated, is deceptively simple. We soon see that there are ups and downs in every relationship, that the closer we are, the farther apart we see ourselves thrown sometimes, that we have to take the rough with the smooth, and we proceed in consequence to take for granted such changes without giving them undue importance. The matter is not so simple as that. The contradictory dealings we see in others are also present in our own behavior, and their roots are deep down in us, too deep for easy observation and ready control. What is more, as we begin to suspect, those flares of obnoxious feelings are not isolated events but a permanent substratum of all our reactions, which acts through them to a greater or lesser degree and endangers with its presence the most important part of our lives, which is our relationships with others. It will pay to observe with further interest the phenomenon in others, the better to gauge its implications when we come to ourselves.

The subjects of our observation have of necessity to be children, as they are spontaneous and innocent enough to let themselves feel what they really feel and to express it with disarming bluntness. Later we learn to veil our feelings and censor our words, and the freshness of our experience is lost in the sophistication of our civilized manners. Children are privileged witnesses of our inner drives, and straightforward exponents of our weaknesses. Here is the case of one such child, surprising in the vehemence of its message, and hurting with the sharpness of its expression.

I was speaking with the parents of a young boy in their home, in the presence of the boy, whose studies and future were precisely the topic of our conversation at the moment, and who kept playing with his toys on the floor while we kept talking and looking at him to check with our eyes the effect our words were having on him. At a point in the proceedings I turned to the boy, and in an attempt to bring him into the discussion that so much concerned him, I asked him the eternal question every boy and girl in this world is asked from the moment he or she has the faculty of speech and the capacity to react to outside inquiry: "What are you going to be when you grow up?" He was following our conversation, and he answered without a moment's hesitation: "I want to be a doctor." The answer already reflected the atmosphere the boy lived in. In the competitive world that awaited him, the medical profession was the surest way to obtain ready employment and acceptable income, and so his parents had expressed the wish that their son would be a doctor, and he had picked up the cue with obedient enthusiasm.

All would have been well if I had stopped at that, but I wanted somehow to prolong the interview, and I went on to ask him a further question without in the least suspecting the trouble I was inviting with it and the embarrassing situation I was going to cause. I asked the boy with a show of interest that charged the trivial question with feigned importance, "And what are you going to do when you are a doctor?" The answer came swift and definite, in clear words and cutting intonation: "When I am a doctor I'll give Daddy and Mommy an injection and I'll kill them!" Daddy and Mommy laughed. I laughed. The boy did not laugh and continued to play with his toys. The interview was over.

Our laughter had covered our embarrassment at the unsuspected onslaught. The boy knew more about the medical profession than his parents had surmised. It was not only a matter of social prestige and worthwhile earnings, but a welcome instrument to get rid of his parents. A quick injection, and the job was done. There was an element of mercy in the boy's fantasy; an injection is painless killing as against the bloodstained violence of a gun or a knife. But the ruthless message was nonetheless there. The boy's favorite daydream was about how to kill his parents. The needle of hatred in the heart of love. The shadow of death in the home of life. Murder in the mind of a child. And unbelieving bewilderment in his well-meaning parents.

The suddenness of the revelation took away our capacity to react in a meaningful and healing way before the attack, and we drowned its message in uneasy laughter. But the boy did not laugh. He had said something serious, and he knew it. He went on playing with his toys and dreaming his dreams. One day he will become a doctor and, his dark dream forgotten, will use all his knowledge and skill to help his parents with any health problem they may have in their old age. But the needle will always be there in the suppressed subconscious, a threat to the intimate relationship and a hidden source of uneasiness, friction, and guilt. A good doctor would remove in time the offending needle from the mind, for better health in the person and happiness in the family.

We would not be so surprised at this incident if we would only remember the many times and ways in which we have seen this negative feeling enacted in home after home. The cases are too many to be cataloged. A boy, holding a toy gun in his hand, approaches his father from behind, points the gun at his head, and shouts with victory in his voice, "Bang, bang! You're dead!" The prank is usually dismissed with a deprecating gesture, a witless rejoinder with another "Bang, bang!", a tired warning that such things are not done, or an irate reminder that the devil loads unloaded guns and we must never play with fire. The obvious meaning of the mock attack is seldom adverted to. The boy is killing his father, releasing in a fit of violence the pent-up feelings of anger and resentment for all the times his father has made him do things he did not want to do, or forbidden him to do things he wanted to do. The grievances add up, the gun is taken, and the mind's dream is enacted in the simplest way the boy has learned from watching it numberless times on the TV screen. The quick trigger, and the smoking gun. The job is over. The mind is relieved from its burden of hatred. And the cycle will start again piling up new grievances and plotting more murders on the home front.

A small girl is pleading before her mother to be taken up in her arms for comfort and care, but her mother is busy, cannot attend to her just now, and tries to explain that to her daughter as lovingly as she can among her sobs and tears. The girl refuses to understand, grows angry, and starts hitting her mother with her closed fists as hard as she can in an unseemly fit of temper. Her small hands cannot physically hurt her mother, but the vicious blows speak clearly their untoward message. She hates her mother. There is no arguing, no reasoning, no bringing to mind all the wonderful good things her mother has done for her and will continue to do with unfailing love; there is now only a wild feeling irrepressibly expressed through a convincing action. The little girl is desperately hitting her mother in a painful display of outward violence. In a way, the girl is wise. By acting out her anger, she gets rid of it, and the next moment she will embrace her mother and rest contentedly in her arms as though nothing had happened. The danger is for the mother, and for us adults on her side, to dismiss the ugly incident as a passing tantrum, and to miss its basic lesson and timely reminder that there are dark emotions within us, and they have to be taken into account if we want to understand well other people's behavior, and better rule our own.

In a lighter vein, I heard once a slightly older girl describe with obvious glee the great time she had had at school that day. She said, her words hardly keeping pace with her enthusiasm in short, breathless sentences, "You know, one of the teachers didn't come today, and the principal came, and she told us we could remain in the classroom by ourselves, only we were not to make noise, and we promised, and then you know what we did? We started criticizing our mommies, one after another, and we all did it, and we had such great fun, and the time passed so quickly, and the principal came again, and congratulated us for behaving so well, and she asked us what we had done, and we didn't tell her, but we had so much fun, so much fun!" The girl was saying all this to her own mother, and she was visibly enjoying saying it. The mother did not enjoy the report so much, and did not ask for the contents of the criticism. If the principal had taped the session, it could have provided matter for fruitful reflection to a group of loving mothers of growing girls.

In some parts of the state where I live in India, the state of Gujarat, transportation of goods is done largely by camel-cart. A caste of camel drivers looks after the patient animals, and the long, solid, sturdy vehicles on inflated tires can be seen on any road as they advance steadily by the side of trucks and cars in happy coexistence of modernity and tradition. The camel driver usually lies down and sleeps on top of the well-packed load while the camel philosophically picks its way and looks down from its vantage point at the speeding, noisy, smoky traffic at his feet. The camel driver delegates most of the responsibility of the trip on the camel, but even so, he has to interfere from time to time. He may have to fit his animal with a muzzle to prevent it from nibbling at the hay piled up on top of the cart in front, may have to pull the reins before an unmanned level-crossing, may urge on an extra mile to reach a convenient resting place for the night.

All that is fine, and the camel knows it, and it is a patient animal; but resentments also pile up within its hump, and when they reach a certain level, they will cause the camel to lose its temper and turn on its driver with teeth and hoof in a highly dangerous way. An enraged camel is a frightful thing indeed. The driver knows it, and he knows the remedy too. Closeness to his silent partner has taught him to gauge the level of resentment within its live sensitivity, and before it reaches the top, he provides a release of the tension without any harm to himself. He takes off his turban, symbol of his caste and protection of his head, and throws it at the feet of the camel. What follows is a spectacle worth watching. The camel jumps on what it knows to be the sign and embodiment of its master, tramples upon it, tears it with its teeth, and reduces it to scattered rags in the frenzy of a wild, savage dance, reminiscent of Shiva's dance for the destruction of the universe. The ritual over, the camel calms down and becomes once again the patient, mild, long-suffering beast of burden to travel uneventfully the long miles of the Indian roads. Its driver, who has watched the proceedings and knows their meaning, gets for himself a new turban and resumes the trade as though nothing had happened. Nothing will disturb the peace of man and beast . . . till a new turban is needed.

The relationship between a camel and its driver seems also to be a love-hate relationship. And goods travel well in Gujarat state.

A Little Red Thread

Parent-child relationships are not the only source for mixed feelings in our lives. In the home itself and in the next-closest dealings of our experience, we find another fertile source of emotional confusion: the relationship between brothers and sisters in the family. *Sibling rivalry* is a consecrated term in our language, and describes with pointed accuracy the contradictory dealings of boys and girls with their brothers and sisters since the beginning of their existence. Here again there is evident love, blood ties, readiness to support and defend each other before outsiders, shared experiences, and treasured memories together. But here also there is friction, jealousy, and downright rivalry in the least admissible but most real competition, which is competition for the parents' attention and love.

The arrival of a small brother or sister in the family signals the first great crisis in a child's life. Till now the firstborn was the center of the home, the hub around which the life of his or her parents turned by day and by night, the first preference at every moment and for every need. And now suddenly the romance is over. The focus is shifted, the privileges abrogated, and the throne vacated for the next incumbent. The child cannot be expected to take his or her own downgrading gracefully, and failure to recognize this on the part of the parents can only aggravate an already serious situation.

When the second child was born to a family of my acquaintance, the first child, who was a two-and-a-half-year-old girl, was sent to stay with her uncles for a month, so that her parents would be more free to welcome the new arrival with due care and full attention. On learning of the arrangements, I made what I thought was an obvious commentary: "The girl must have felt her exile for the month." But they remonstrated with me and stressed that they had foreseen it all and had taken good care to instruct and prepare the girl to accept the new situation at home. "She is a very understanding girl for her age, and we have explained everything to her carefully. She knows that a little brother is coming, that he is small and will require constant attention the first days he is at home, just as she required when she came. So it is good for her and for her brother that she goes for a few days, and she has seen it so and is quite willing to go and has said so. There will be no problem."

There *was* a problem. After the first week, the uncles phoned from their place. The girl was restless, she had lost appetite and developed a fever, and was talking the whole time about going back home. She had to be rescued the next day, and she came, with no fever and a healthy appetite, and with an eager look to find out how things had changed at home during her absence, whether her position was safe, and what she could expect now in the changed environment. Adapting to a new brother or sister is no easy task, and by ignoring this fact, we can only harm those concerned. The conflict situation can be changed, and the original mistrust can become, with time and guidance and constant goodwill, genuine support and intimate closeness; but the first step toward solving the conflict is recognizing its existence.

Doris Brett, in *Annie Stories*, makes this point graphically clear.

> Suddenly, one evening, your husband comes home. "Darling!" he shouts. "I have wonderful news!" "Yes?" you respond eagerly. Has he bought tickets to Acapulco? A honeymoon hideaway on Hawaii? A romantic rendezvous in Paris? You wait eagerly for his reply. You know it must be something very special because he is so excited. You haven't seen him so excited since the day you got married. What ever can it be? "Yes, darling," he says, "wonderful news! I've brought home a new wife!" As you attempt to regain consciousness, your husband continues. "Because she's new, she'll need a lot of special attention, so I'll be moving her into our own bedroom, and you can sleep out in the study. I'm dying for you to see her. She's so young and sweet and helpless—you'll just adore her. Because she doesn't know much yet, she's going to need a lot of my time, but I know you won't mind that—you're such a mature, competent person, you don't really need me all that much. And I know you're going to love taking care of her and sharing your clothes and friends and make-up with her. You're just going to adore her! Aren't you excited, darling! Darling? Darl . . . ? Aaaargh!" Enough said?*

The analogy is clear. The newcomer is looked upon as an intruder, and it is from there that the treatment should start. To tell the older child how wonderful it will be with the new brother or sister, how they will play together and love each other at first sight, is misleading and unhelpful. Such an approach will only

* Doris Brett, *Annie Stories* (New York: Workman Publishing, 1988), p. 85.

induce a sense of guilt in the older child, who cannot come up to the expectation placed upon him or her. On the contrary, it will be wise to allow the expression of angry feelings, which will do less harm by being expressed before understanding parents, and can so be transformed with patience and skill into genuine family affection. To take reality into account is the best way to cope with it.

Sibling tension continues through the years, as the children contend for preferential treatment at the hands of their parents. Any parental decision in favor of one of them will kindle jealousy in the other, and the unavoidable friction will cause alternate feelings and passing moods. The interesting point to note is that it is not only the supposedly rejected child who can be prey to an unhealthy feeling, but also, and paradoxically, the victorious opponent. The reason is not hard to see. The child who sees him or herself preferred to a brother or sister may feel that he or she has let the sibling down, may be burdened with a sense of betrayal and be oppressed by guilt, particularly if the situation is repeated and a complex emerges. Victory can be as damaging as defeat when there is question of the inside of the human heart, which may find a triumph over a close blood relation more difficult to bear than one's own defeat.

The point is that the passing sense of hatred is never alone, but is inserted and surrounded and permeated by love, and thus the instant viciousness of crushing a brother or sister is immediately and deeply followed by the real pain, sorrow, and repentance for having stepped over one's own blood. In this reaction lies the fundamental message of hope that the love-hate relationship brings with itself: It tells us not so much that there is hatred in the midst of love, but that there is love in the midst of hatred, and that even the worst affective conflict can resolve itself and make way for reconciliation and friendship. And so it happens in life so many times. What is important here is not to ignore the hatred, sweep it under the rug and forget about it. If the unworthy feeling is thus forcibly silenced, it will surface again and cause havoc in its time, while it can be healed and neutralized if kept within sight and dealt with wisely.

Freud takes a practical view of this transformation of sibling rivalry into brotherly and sisterly love. Here is his analysis:

> The bigger boy would, out of jealousy, do away with his smaller brother, would remove him from his parents' sight and deprive him of all his rights; but faced with the positive fact that this smaller brother—as indeed all that come after him—is equally loved by the parents, and realizing that he cannot, without harm to himself, maintain his own hostile attitude, our little hero is forced to identify with the rest of the children, and a group feeling is formed in the family circle, a feeling that will later reach a further development in the school. The first demand of this social reaction is justice and equal dealings for all. The strength and unanimity with which this claim shows itself in the school are well-known. Since I cannot be the favored one, let at least no one be. This transformation of jealousy into group feeling in the children of a family or the pupils of a school would seem unlikely if we would not observe exactly the same process at a later stage and under different circumstances. It is enough to remember the number of women and girls who fall romantically in love with a singer or a pianist, and crowd round him at the end of a concert. Each one of them could be perfectly right in feeling jealous of all the others; yet, given their number and the consequent impossibility of monopolizing the beloved one, they all give up their claim, and instead of pulling out one another's hair, they act as a concerted crowd, they offer to their idol the common worship, and even consider themselves happy if they can distribute among themselves the golden curls of his precious hair. They were rivals for a start, but the even love they feel for the same person has allowed them to

> become one among themselves. When an instinctive situation can give rise to different endings—as it happens in fact in most of them—there is no wonder if the one that brings with itself a certain satisfaction is the one that actually takes place, instead of others we thought were more natural, but were barred by the actual circumstances. *

Freud had a sense of humor, as this passage makes clear, and would have smiled if he had watched the crowds at a rock concert, and the scenes of popular devotion and plain hysterics that take place before the rock star with predictable regularity. He takes a pragmatic view of human nature, and sets on record its capacity to turn an unfavorable situation into a favorable one. It almost looks like the familiar advice "If you can't beat them, join them!" This approach seems to imply that the first feeling was one of hostility, and only later did friendship grow out of it. But this need not be so. In fact, it seems more according to the order of things that the love comes first, between parents and children as between brothers and sisters. The first feeling that is learned through instinct and immediacy, through atmosphere and environment, is the one of belonging, of being close, of a special relationship to those who live together in a place called home. Children like their parents, and children like their brothers and sisters as organic reaction to the blood in their veins and the kinship in their senses. Only then, as friction induced by the very closeness, will the adverse traits appear and inaugurate the struggle. This is why it becomes possible and, given the circumstances, surprisingly easy to return to the original love and strengthen it as life matures.

Doris Brett, whom I quoted at the beginning of this chapter, writes on in the same passage:

* *Sigmund Freud, Massenpsychologie und Ich-Analyse*, p. 57. Published in English as *Group Psychology and the Analysis of the Ego* (New York: W. W. Norton, 1975).

> Perhaps the astonishing thing about sibling relationships is
> not that they contain so much negativity, but that so many
> siblings are able to touch their relationships with the Phi-
> losopher's Stone—that magic transformer which alchemists
> believed was able to turn base metal into gold. Out of the
> darker emotions of jealousy, greed, fear, and anger, they
> can bring forth altruism, generosity, supportiveness, love.
> Such a transformation does not happen magically, of
> course. It requires time and effort on the part of the
> siblings—support and understanding on the part of the par-
> ents. *

In India there is a beautiful custom I have witnessed year after
year, learning every time a little more about its tradition and its
practice. In the yearly festival of *Rakshabandhan* on the day of
Barev, when the Brahmans change their sacred thread, there is
another rite practiced in every home where there is a brother and
sister of whatever age. The sister will come in the morning, call
her brother, and tie a red thread around his right wrist. Then she
will touch his head with her right hand in blessing, and will
receive with a hug and a happy laugh the gift her brother has kept
ready for her. Every sister will do that to every brother of hers,
and that day the proud red band will adorn the hands of all those
men in town who are lucky enough to have a sister. If the sister
lives elsewhere, she will send the thread by mail well in time, so
that the brother will not be deprived of the sisterly blessing. Most
people untie the thread the next day, but loving brothers who
know the ancient rubrics keep it for two months until the festival
of *Dassera*, when the thread is officially removed. Thus brothers
and sisters are the center of these two important festivals.

And there is still a third festival, *Bhaibij*, which is the second
day of the Hindu year, in which the brother eats only the meal
cooked and served him personally by his sister. If the sister lives

* Doris Brett, *Annie Stories.*

in another place, he will go to her house to be entertained by her, as the best way to begin the new year. These customs show how firmly established is the sister-brother relationship in the Indian tradition.

The red thread around the wrist is a sign of protection, almost a seal of ownership that marks the brother and defends him against all adverse forces in this hostile world. It is like the king's ring on a messenger's hand, to signify that he is the king's messenger and nobody can touch him, as that would be an offense against the king himself. The sister, with the right that her womanhood, her beauty, and her love give her as fairy queen in a magic world, sets her seal on her brother as protection and blessing, while the brother swears in turn to stand by his sister through life with his love, his strength, and his care. The red thread becomes symbol and reminder of the model love that prepares the human heart, with comfort and support, for the struggles that make up life on earth. That boy will soon learn how to call all girls of his acquaintance "sisters," and the girl will call all boys "brothers," in consistent linguistic testimony, alive today in India, to the best of feelings in the loveliest of ways. As a consequence, the boy will seek a bride outside his village, since all the girls in his village are his "sisters," and this custom will foster the broadening of the village's horizons, and the establishing of blood relationship with other villages, as is happily done still today.

One year, on occasion of the feast of the thread, the newspapers carried a surprising news item, emphasized by a front-page photograph. In the course of the preceding year a man had been murdered, and the murderer had been caught, judged, and sentenced to a jail term he was then serving. On the day of the festival of the thread, the murdered man's widow had visited the jail, and had tied, as a sign of forgiveness and reconciliation, the red thread on the right wrist of the man who had murdered her husband. She knew herself, by conviction and tradition, a sister to all men, even to the one who had brought sorrow to her life, and manifested now in the traditional ritual the generosity of her heart. Touching expression of the lofty ideal that makes all men my brothers and all women my sisters.

I was so moved by this beautiful custom when I first observed it in India that I wrote a whole chapter about it in one of my first books in the language of the land. The chapter was made up of two talks I had given on that inspiring subject, one in a university hostel for boys, and the other in a similar institution for girls. At the end I mused in a final paragraph that as I had no sister in my own family, I was given now to understand and feel these deep social and moral values vicariously through the practice of others, and there was no red thread on my right wrist on the festival day. I was still a newcomer to India when I wrote that, and I had underestimated the feminine response. When the next festival of the thread came around, the mail brought me so many red threads that they would have covered my whole arm, had I tried to tie them all. As I could not tie them all, I tied none; and then, not without some wistful regret, I proceeded to cancel that last paragraph in all subsequent editions of the book.

One thread, I did accept in person. I was staying with a Hindu family when the feast came around, and the girl in the house approached her brother for the ceremony. I watched the proceedings and waited. I had observed that the girl had brought not one thread but two. When she had finished, she turned toward me and remained silent. I also remained silent, and extended my right hand toward her. She tied the thread. I was going to say that I had no gift ready for her, when she, who seemed to have foreseen everything, told me boldly, "All I want is that you keep it till *Dassera.*" I said, "I will." On the next day I went to address my mathematics class in the college as usual, and when I turned to the blackboard and began writing equations with my extended right hand, I sensed a murmur sweep through the class. The students had spotted the red thread and were wondering who could have tied it. I let them wonder. The sanctity of mathematics cannot be stained with personal considerations. But I kept my promise and wore with pride the sisterly blessing till its final day. I also need protection in this difficult world. And I was glad to have been initiated into the noble heritage that extends to all men and women the strong and tender relationship of brothers and sisters in the family. One more reason for me to try to understand, deepen, and purify all family relationships, primary source of our intimate welfare.

A White Handkerchief

It is significant that our first examples of love-hate relationships should have been children. Their social innocence makes them transparent and outspoken, much to the embarrassment of their parents and the amusement of everybody else. They have not yet learned to hide their feelings from people around them, much less to hide them from themselves as later they will do with unfailing efficiency to the detriment of their liveliness and spontaneity. They are still open and playful, and their reactions are faithful reflections of their feelings.

Soon they will lose their innocence. This is not done. This is not said. Be civil. Be polite. Smile when you feel like smirking. Thank people when you feel like cursing them. Show interest when you have none. Appear to listen when your mind is miles away. Wear the mask. Play the game. That is what all do, and that is the way to survive in a world of strife and competition where no information is given about oneself, to ward off competitors and preserve safety. Secret is the soul of business, say those who know, and smoke screens or scrambling devices are widely used in battle and in life. Let no one know what I really think, so that they cannot put obstacles in my way before I even begin to walk.

The trouble with smoke screens is that they work both ways. The smoke I produce gets into my own eyes, and eventually my own vision is blurred. By not allowing others to see me as I really am, I end up not seeing it myself; that is, I do not see myself as I really am. I lose contact with myself, I come to believe that I am quite different from what I am in fact. I hide from myself some of the dark corners of my personality to spare myself the pain of facing them, and I come to think honestly that in spite of weaknesses and shortcomings which I certainly have and admit, I am free from serious vices or notable failings I hear and read are common in others. One such dark corner is the "hate" part in the love-hate relationships. I know about that, but I sincerely think it does not apply to me. I do not hate anybody, least of all those who are closest to me in gratitude and affection. Yes, I know that such things happen to others, and I have read about them in psychology manuals; but no, that is not my case, thanks, and I do not feel the need to go further into it. We can safely leave it at that, and I would like it so.

Once a young woman came to see me. She was studying for her Ph.D. at the university where I was teaching. She came from a respected family and was well bred in everything. In the course of her story, she told me how much she loved her parents, how she owed to them everything she was, how she could not even think of disobeying them or in any way causing them pain. There was, of course, the present matter that was on her mind and very much on her heart, her parents' refusal to let her marry the boy she loved. That was painful for her, to be sure, but she understood. She loved them very much and she owed them everything she had. So she had already told the boy that it was impossible for her to continue with him, and she had severed the relationship. Even in her pain, she was satisfied and happy that she had done the "right" thing.

Her words were dutiful, restrained, refined. She was not dissembling or hiding the truth in any conscious way. She was saying what she thought she felt, what she had disciplined herself to feel. She hated her parents for not allowing her to marry the boy she loved, but she would not say it, would not permit herself to think it. She would not allow herself to acknowledge the resentment against her parents, however justified this might have been, that she did so deeply feel.

If I had merely listened to her words, I would have followed her reasoning and identified with her feelings. Her voice was calm, her mood recollected, her whole attitude self-possessed and dignified and proper. In her love for her parents, she had responsibly chosen the way that pleased them. That was what she said, and that was what her words clearly meant.

But as she took considerable time with her story, my eyes had the opportunity to wander on their own, and after a while they settled inquisitively on her hands. Those lovely hands were doing quite an act of their own. In them she held a small, dainty handkerchief, as many girls indeed do for some unfathomable reason when they come to talk about their lives. As she warmed up in her narrative, her hands began to busy themselves with the handkerchief. What they did to that perfumed and embroidered little fabric was worth watching, and I did so, first with amusement and then with growing uneasiness and discomfort. She was twisting the handkerchief, squeezing it, wringing it out of shape. As she was saying "I love my parents so much . . ." her hands were torturing the white little square with relentless fury. "I could not even imagine how I could do anything that would cause my parents any pain . . ." she went on, as her hands strangled to death the helpless handkerchief in ritual execution. Delicate hands in their deadly errand. As she went on, mindless in her words of what she was doing with her hands.

Her hands were free. Censorship had not reached them. They had escaped the vigilant eye of the conscious mind. They moved on their own to express the hidden truth of the uncensored subconscious. And they did it with a vengeance. They tortured, twisted, throttled, as the voice kept on singing its docile monotone. The demure girl and the ruthless executioner, the nurtured reaction and the wild fury, the obedience and the revolution. A split-screen demonstration of the conflicting tides that sway the human heart.

I watched the painful act with a heavy heart. I let it run its course, let the words repeat platitudes and the hands spell their doom. Finally there was silence. I waited still a little, and then said with as much tenderness as I could bring to my voice, to soften the blow of the naked realization with the concern of a fellow sufferer, "Do you realize that you would like to do to your parents what you are doing to your handkerchief?" She looked at her hands, saw the shapeless rag that had been her handkerchief, gasped in horror, and began to cry. No explanation was needed. Her hands had spoken, and she had read the message. She knew it all along, but had forcibly withdrawn from her consciousness the painful admission of the improper feeling. And the repressed violence had turned on herself and done harm to the tender makeup of her soul. Hatred is poison, and not finding a surgically clean outlet, it had turned on her and stinted her youth. A little handkerchief had saved her from further damage. Maybe that is why girls bring a handkerchief in their hands when they come to speak of their troubles.

*   *   *

Here is the telling experience of a sensitive and intelligent woman in dialogue with her psychoanalyst (John).

Suddenly a scene flashed into memory, forgotten for twenty-one years. I stood alone in the street outside my school. January's ice-wind snapped in from the water. I waited for Mother to pick me up, as she usually did, to drive me home for lunch. I was still there, long after lunch hour, my face blood-red from the cold. A teacher walked by, asked why I stood in the street. "My mother's forgotten me," I told her, teeth chattering. She led me indoors. She found out Mother had telephoned, asking that I eat at school as she was unable to call for me. The switchboard girl had neglected to tell me. As apology the school fed me a mammoth meal including double dessert. But that could not remove the hurt in my heart. I was convinced Mother had finally forsaken me. I lived through the experience once more, describing it to John. As I put it into words a strange thing happened. I started to sob and could not stop. I sobbed as though making up for all the tears I could not shed that day I felt abandoned. And the words that came out in anger to my amazement were: "Why did she hate me so? What did I do to her that she should hate me?" "She didn't hate you," he answered softly. "Yes, she did," I insisted. "My mother hated me. And I hated her!" I stopped, stunned. What was I saying? What right had he to pull out feelings better left unrevealed? No nice girl should hate her mother or feel her mother hates her. Nice girls are brought up to respect parents, not to answer them back or alarm them or make them unhappy. Besides, I hated no one. I tried to love everyone. Hate inside me? Never. Yet, how could I, who demanded explanation for everything, explain why, in one unguarded moment, I felt I had exposed a dart of hatred once hurled at me that had remained quivering inside ever since?*

* Lucy Freeman, *Fight Against Fears* (New York: Continuum, 1988), p. 44.

Nice girls do not oppose their parents or do anything to make them unhappy. Hate inside me? Never! Yet there it was. For twenty-one years. Buried under layers of conformity, good manners, propriety, dignity. Censored out of consciousness by the unfailing discipline of an exemplary daughter. But very much present and alive in the dark recesses of the soul, embittering and poisoning from there every thought and feeling and action and relationship with all the greater efficiency as its source remained hidden and its influence unknown. We all carry within ourselves such memories, such resentments, such hatred, and our refusal to acknowledge them hurts us with the safe impunity of the disguised foe.

Many dark moods, many despondent feelings, many unaccountable irritations, many disproportionate quarrels, have their occult roots in the festering subsoil of our neglected frustrations. We stiffen ourselves to conform to accepted standards, to measure up to expectations, to play our assigned roles, to wear the mask and to veil our true faces even before we look at ourselves in the mirror. We come to believe in our smile and to trust in our goodness. We have our failings, to be sure, but our heart is clean and our feelings noble. Far from us any base emotion or any mean judgment. We are fair in our opinions and loving in our dealings. Or so we think. The reality can be different, and our blindness to recognize it can do great harm to the balance and health of our lives. Censorship cripples information, and crippled information leads to crippled behavior.

We cancel the word *hate* from our personal vocabulary. We do not hate people. We never do such a thing. If the other person is particularly obnoxious, unpleasant, repellent, and generally intolerable, we may say that we dislike, avoid, reject, steer clear of, that person, and would not be seen in his or her company for all the money in the world. But we do not hate anyone. To hate is unchristian, unethical, unacceptable, and when we gratefully and responsibly accept the divine command to love even our enemies and those who do us harm, we effectively distance ourselves from any feeling or manifestation of the condemned passion. We do not hate anyone.

Curiously enough, the banished word does show up in our conversation, seeking milder contexts, but asserting in a way its presence in our memory and its readiness on our lips. We easily say things like, "I hate raw onions!" "I hate TV commercials!" "I hate getting wet in the rain!" It is understandable that we dislike onions or commercials or getting soaked on our way to work, but the expression seems greatly to exceed the inconvenience experienced. Put the onion aside, change the TV channel by just pressing a key in the remote control, or buy an umbrella and hold it over your head while you walk. There is certain unpleasantness involved, to be sure, but none of those situations, and of many such in our lives, is the proper and proportionate setting for such a strong feeling as formal hatred. The word is filed up in our personal computer, as the feeling is locked up in our hearts; and as their appearance in weighty contexts is banned, they show up in lighter moments to assert their presence and renew their touch. The word is still in our vocabulary because the feeling is still in our hearts. Consider this story from Kahlil Gibran's *The Madman*, tragic in its realism and almost cruel in its briefness. He calls it "The Sleepwalkers":

> In the town of my birth there lived a woman and her daughter, and both walked in their sleep. One night, while silence shrouded the earth, the woman and her daughter walked fully asleep, till they met in a garden under the cover of heavy mist.
>
> The mother was the first to speak. "At last!" she said. "At last I can tell you what I always wanted to say! Yes, to tell

you who destroyed my youth, and are now building your own life on the ruins of mine! I want to kill you!"

Then it was the daughter's turn to speak, and these were her words: "Oh hateful woman, selfish and decrepit! You come between my freedom and my self! You would like my life to be but an echo of your own withered life! I wish you were dead!"

At that moment the cock crowed, and both women woke up. "Is that you, my treasure?" said the mother tenderly. "Yes, it is me, dearest mother," answered the daughter with equal tenderness.

Sleep reveals the secrets of the mind. The dire words are spoken under cover of night. The burden is temporarily lifted, and the subconscious relieved for a while. But the cock crows and the curtain is drawn. Darkness thickens in the graves of time.

If we live long enough, old age may bring a second childhood, and some of our lifelong inhibitions can be removed. Permanent controls may loosen up as memory fails, willpower weakens, and the bonds of self-discipline slacken with the waning of conscious faculties. That is how old age can bring back childhood innocence, and the censorship of a lifetime can be lifted in its last stage. And this is why feelings of hatred, freely felt and expressed in the first years of life, and repressed later in deference to civility and morals, surface again in old age and find marked expression which shocks and bewilders those who witness the outbursts, and often also shocks the very person who stages the display. The Uruguayan writer Eduardo Galeano gives a telling example of his experience. In "The Grandmother," he tells an actual incident in the life of a real person he knew well:

Bertha Jensen's grandmother died cursing. She had lived all her life walking on tiptoe, as though apologizing for her presence, dedicated to the service of her husband and her

five children; exemplary wife, devoted mother, silent model
of feminine virtue: never a complaint left her lips, let alone
a harsh word. When sickness struck her, she called her
husband, made him sit on her bed, and began. Nobody
suspected she knew the vocabulary of a drunken sailor. The
agony lasted long. For more than a month, grandmother
vomited from her bed a steady stream of insults and blas-
phemies straight from the filthiest gutter. Even her voice
had changed. She, who had never smoked or drunk anything beyond water or milk, swore now with a hoarse voice.
Thus, cursing, she died. And there was general relief in the
family and in the neighborhood. *

I have known such cases in my own experience. Too many,
unfortunately, to be considered as isolated cases. Holy men and
women of proven virtue and model lives, who, on reaching old
age, lose by sheer nervous decay the iron control that had sus-
tained their upright characters, and, to their own and everybody's
distress, let loose a flow of unseemly language to which there
seems to be no end. Once I found a holy old priest doing just that
while leaning precariously on the half-open door of his sickroom
in the old people's infirmary. He had held responsible jobs as
rector, superior, and provincial throughout his life, going from
one post to another from the moment he finished his studies till
the protracted end of his active life. Maybe, on reflection, the
very tensions he undoubtedly had to endure in the exercise of his
governing duties tensed his nerves, taxed his patience, and loaded
resentments in his breast, which was accustomed to keeping secrets. Dark feelings were safe in the personal archives of the
responsible religious. All his life he had been considered a living
picture of the rules and regulations to be observed; he was punc-
tual, active, devout, prayerful, considerate, modest, reliable, fair,
generous, persevering, thoughtful. The embodiment of the per-

* Eduardo Galeano, *El libro de los abrazos* (Madrid: Siglo XXI Editores, 1989), p. 220.

fect religious. As such, he was honored and respected by all who
knew him and lived under him or heard about him. And his
reputation accompanied him wherever he went in his long and
eventful career.

All would have been well if he had died in time. Even in his
retirement he had kept his dignity, his flawless habits and pleasant manners; and his lifelong reputation enhanced his venerable
figure wherever he went. But he lived one year too long. One
year before his death, something snapped in the tightly super-
vised controls of his regulated life. The lid went off the chest of
secrets. The tongue was loosened, and the resentments of a lifetime began to flow in an unholy tide of frightful proportions. I
had heard about it, and that day I was an unwary victim of the
outrageous onslaught. As soon as he spotted me at one end of the
long corridor, he motioned me to come close, held my shirt with
one hand while he supported himself on the door with the other,
and unleashed the verbal punishment. He said with jarring voice
and twisted features, "You all want to get rid of me, isn't that it?
I know it. But you will not succeed. I will not die. You will have
to keep looking after me, whether you like it or not. I know that
you hate me for the things you have to do to me now; but I also
hated you all my life for the nuisance you all were to me wherever I was. Go and tell them all: I mean to be around still for
quite some time, and I will have my vengeance making you look
after me in all my needs as I had to put up with all of you and
your stupidities for so many years."

I listened with a mixture of pity, sorrow, and astonishment.
The great man had accumulated so much dirt in his repressed
memory along his long career that at length the dam had burst
and the flood would not now be stemmed. The mixed feelings
had been there through life. The good ones had been acknowledged with gratitude and humility, and the bad ones had been

suppressed with energy. That was the regular training of a sturdy
generation. Its effects were noteworthy for a time, but the heroic
scheme broke down in the end and the secret was out. There was
no question of any blame in the man, who had faithfully followed the training he was given in the stern tradition of his time,
and had seen his self-control collapse through sheer mental fa-
tigue in the cogwheels of his weary mind. But there was certainly
the loving regret in all those who had known him in his days of
greatness, and witnessed now the disintegration of a lofty mind.
There had been negative feelings in him all along, but by ignoring them and shelving them, he had only prepared the tragic
showdown of his last days. Negative feelings can be ignored only
at a price.

I do not say all this to harp on the weaknesses or failings of great
people. I say it purely and simply because I do not want this to
happen to me. I do not want to blow my top in my old age, if I
ever reach it, and even if I do not reach it, I do not want to carry
through life the unhappy burden of hidden resentments and secret hatred. I want to clean dark corners, sweep below the carpet,
air grievances, confess animosities. I want to face the mixture
within me, face the angel and the devil in me, the genial companion and the shameless rogue, the genuine well-wisher and the
mean backbiter. If I pride myself on being a kind lover, I must
realize that I also can be at times an ignoble hater. Only by airing
my house in time can I avoid being choked by my own smoke
when it is too late. I do not want to die cursing.

"Please, Tell Someone . . ."

The importance of relationships in our life is that they literally shape us. We come into this world with an inherited makeup that will mark the directions of our growth and the limits of our development. That is the raw matter on which the events and circumstances of our environment set to work. They bring out our possibilities and direct our course, they enkindle our desires and drive them to completion . . . or to frustration as the case may be. Outside influences have much to say on what we are going to be, the kind of person we are going to grow into. Inheritance and environment are the two great factors that mold our lives.

Among the external factors, the chief ones are persons. We are born into history and society, and history and society are made up of men and women with their ideas and feelings and dreams and prejudices. And all that is communicated to us through word and gesture, through intimate conversation or public propaganda.

Parents and relatives, teachers and preachers, friends and acquaintances, approach us, deal with us, leave their mark on us
through their words and example, their advice and criticism,
their views and gossip. Everything counts, everything tells on us,
and the clue to much of what we think and do in later life is to
be found in the early influence of persons close to us. The list of
persons who have surrounded us at different periods in our lives
is essential to understanding our personal biography.

As our personality is varied and complex, we need different
persons in our lives to respond to the different aspects of our
character. We may find one friend more amenable to discussing
our ideas with him or her, while another may be a genial companion in games but may not respond to an intellectual exchange
of any kind. One friendship may be more affective, another more
entertaining, a third one more cerebral. We like to joke with
some of our friends, and to be serious with others. In fact, one
good way to measure the closeness of a friendship is to see how
many aspects it covers, how many facets of our personality are
reflected in that friend, in how many of the circumstances of life
we seek his or her company. We are many things to many people, and the more things we are to one particular individual, the
closer will he or she be to us, and we to him or her. The ideal
friend covers all our life with his or her affection, understanding,
patience, silence, conversation, sympathy, criticism, partnership
in games, company in travels, care in sickness, echo in laughter.
The more of our life we can share with a single individual, the
more intimate the friendship will be; and since often we may not
find that universal response in one person, we widen the range of
our friendship and open up different angles of our life to different
people who fit into them and complete between them the circle
of intimacy we need for our happiness and well-being. We know

our different faces, and are glad to show them to those who like them and know and appreciate us through them.

The telephone rings. I pick up the receiver and speak into it the single noncommittal word "Yes?" with a neutral intonation to cover the origin of any possible call without committing myself or revealing my identity. When the caller identifies himself or herself, I react immediately with pointed clarity according to the person I know I am speaking with. I say, "I'm Carlos" or "I'm Father Valles" or "I'm Carlos Gonzales Valles" as the case may be. I am defining myself from the start in a different way according to the person I address; the tone of voice, the phrasing of each expression, the choice of words, and the speed of my speech vary as I think of the face that is addressing the receiver at the other end of the line. I am different things to different people, and my telephone knows it.

The best case in my telephone experience is that of a former bishop of my diocese. He answered his phone himself, as in his poverty and simplicity he had no secretary, and whoever the caller might be, he invariably answered in the same tone of voice with the following words: "This is number 24717." His official status prevented any preferences, distinctions, or closeness to anyone, and so he just stated his number and proclaimed his aloofness. He could not say, "I am the bishop" in a Hindu city where most of his people do not know what a bishop is; and he could not just familiarly give his name when the caller could be a Catholic who would not expect such chumminess from the highest authority in the diocese. So the impersonal number was the proper answer: 24717. That was the actual number. And it signified and expressed the impartiality and evenness and equal love of the universal pastor toward all the sheep of his flock. He had assumed his official personality, and lived it out with exemplary logic.

Another telephone anecdote, I experienced in a certain African country while on a lecture tour to the Indian community there. I observed that when the phone rang in their homes, or even when I called from one home to another, the very first words they pronounced, before having time to listen to anything from the other end, were in their own Indian language. They did not expect calls from "outsiders," and spoke from the start in their own language, knowing that the answer, too, would come in that language. Here again the self-definition of the person who answered the phone was simplified by the assumption of the nature of the caller, and one language covered all situations. In each case, the personality was defined and shaped by the way it appeared before others.

The phone is only an example. Every face, every greeting, every letter, every encounter, draws a different card from our pack, plays on a different string, elicits a different response. We find ourselves in contrast and interaction with all the people we meet in life, particularly those who are closer to us and stay longer in contact. Relationships form the chisel that carves out our image.

This also means that without a chisel, there will be no statue. Without relationships, there is no personality. Or, at most, a stunted and coarse personality. Lack of relationships means isolation, distance, solitude. Such a desert existence may be interesting for a while, but in the long run will yield only sand and dunes. A certain amount of solitude is unavoidable in human life, and can even contribute to the molding of character in the sternness of our existence. It is remarkable that two Nobel prize-winning authors of our day have as their main works two books with the word *solitude* in their titles and indeed in their arguments: Octavio Paz's *The Labyrinth of Solitude*, and Gabriel

García Márquez's A *Hundred Years of Solitude.* In the words of
Octavio Paz:

> Solitude is the final layer of the human condition. All our
> efforts tend to abolish solitude. To feel lonely has a double
> meaning; on the one hand it is taking conscience of our
> Self; and on the other, longing to get out of the Self. Sol-
> itude, which is the very climate of our lives, appears as a test
> and a purification, at the end of which anguish and inse-
> curity will disappear. The fullness and encounter, which
> are repose and bliss and reconciliation with the world, await
> us at the end of the labyrinth of solitude. *

Paradoxically we can say that the art of living consists of going
through the unavoidable labyrinth of solitude . . . in good company. Solitude will be ours without looking for it. In the midst of
a crowd and in the darkness of a night, in the din of a party and
in the silence of a morning walk. We are alone and we know it,
even when we are discussing our loneliness with someone else,
who feels as lonely as we do in the exchange. The effort is now
to redeem solitude into encounter, monologue into dialogue, the
single point into the cosmic space. To find the social dimension
of our lives in the midst of our confirmed individuality. To reach
the circumference without leaving the center. To enlarge horizons without losing their unifying perspective. To realize in
thought and in deed that to be ourselves, we have to meet others,
and to grow to full stature, we need the companionship of all
those who grow around us and with us.

Isolation deforms a person. It involves loss of touch with reality, loss of feedback from fellow human beings, loss of opportu-
nities to check one's bearings and correct one's course. And if the
isolation is prolonged, the harm may be beyond remedy. The

* Octavio Paz, *The Labyrinth of Solitude* (Madrid: Collección Popular, 1990), p. 237.

contact broken, or never established, remains broken; the more time elapses, the harder it becomes to mend the breach, and the isolation becomes confirmed, hardened, settled. If the malady strikes deep roots, it remains for life and cripples the person. There are such cases along the roads of life.

Without judging, and much less condemning, anyone, with full respect to each one's individuality and idiosyncrasies, and recognizing that a deformed character may hide a sterling soul, I remember here some cases I have personally known in which a lifelong isolation has brought pain, distortion, and frustration to the persons concerned and all those who loved them. They were people who lived with others, to be sure, in the midst of a group, of society, of a life of meetings and contacts and rubbing shoulders with other people in daily social exchange; but for some reason unknown to others, and most likely to themselves, or for no reason at all, they distanced themselves, they set up boundaries, they withdrew to themselves and avoided contacts. Initial shyness, early frictions, mistrust, fear, wrong understanding of imagined duty, affective laziness, or stinginess with their time. Something happened, an attitude was taken, an image projected, a behavior reinforced, a custom acquired. And the lonely person became officially and publicly lonely. No friends, no affection, no intimacy. The haughty stand of the self-sufficient individual. As he kept his distance from others, others kept their distance from him, and the separation was sealed. The person moved in society, but without belonging to it, without mixing with it or being touched by it. The lack of dialogue made his speech one-sided, and the lack of contrasting views made his vision blurred.

I have in mind some of those people who, not lacking in intellectual qualities and wide information, took to writing with scholarship and authority. But their flaw showed. People who knew them and read their published writings wondered how they could have resorted to cynicism in their arguments or meanness in their judgments. Pitiful print among worthy research. Unhappy shoot from embittered roots. Defacing blot in innocent pages. Noble lives twisted into dysfunction by the blight of protracted isolation. Pointed reminder of the absolute need of relationships and friendships to grow in normality and balance and wisdom and health. Without others, we cannot be ourselves.

Eduardo Galeano, whom I quoted previously, records in the same book another telling anecdote on the loneliness of men and women. "Some times, at the end of the season, when the tourists left Calella, one could hear howlings and wailings from the mountain. They came from dogs that had been tied to the trees on the side of the mountain. The tourists had used those dogs to relieve their own solitude during their sojourn in the holidays; and later, at the time of leaving, they tied them far into the mountain that they might not follow them" (p. 172). Forlorn image of human dereliction. A noble animal as companion to make up for the lack of human warmth in life. The person who has found no solace in fellow human beings turns to the fidelity and trustworthiness of the loyal animal.

Respect for animal life, appreciation of the lively role of all animals in the garden of creation, ecological concern for their protection and well-being, are positive values to be prized and fostered for the good of all beings under heaven. But a dog can never be a substitute for a human friend. A woman told me once, pointing to her dog, "My dog will never let me down; men and women often have." With that sentence, she justified her attachment to her dog and her withdrawing from all human relationships. That was a sharp, and not entirely unmerited, criticism of the thoughtless way in which we men and women often behave with people we call friends; and it was at the same time a just recognition of the outstanding virtue of mankind's best nonhuman companion. But that does not justify the willful ostracism of a person into affective exile. Again a man told me: "When I get back home daily in the evening, I can be sure of receiving an enthusiastic welcome from my dog . . . but not always from my wife." This might be true, but if it were to lead to partiality to the dog over the wife, the husband would only cause harm to himself and to his family. The answer, both for the disappointed husband and for the betrayed woman in the previous example, does not lie in withdrawing from humans and resorting to dogs, but in working out the reasons for the existing conflicts; in looking at the possible flaws in themselves that cause the unfriendly reactions in others; in accepting the limitations of reality and realizing that even so, the companionship of a like-minded person is far more rewarding in exchange of thoughts and birth of feelings than the caresses of the loveliest animal.

It is unfair for the tourists to tie the dogs to trees; but the original misdeed was that they endeared the dogs to themselves as a temporary and easily available substitute for human affection, knowing that at the end of the season, they would abandon them. Repeated loneliness had led those men and women to a behavior unworthy of the human race. The solution lay in reconciling themselves to humankind and returning to the fold in time. We do not want the pain and the shame of the night howlings of the derelict dogs on the side of the mountain in the fashionable summer resort. Innocent victims of human loneliness.

The same writer, Eduardo Galeano, tells an even more poignant experience of heartrending loneliness.

> Fernando Silva runs a children's hospital in Managua. On Christmas Eve he stayed in it with his work late into the night. Rockets were already bursting in the air, and fireworks had begun to light up the sky when Fernando finally got up to leave. At home they were waiting for him to

celebrate the feast. He had a last look at the several wards, satisfied himself that everything was in order, and while he was thus walking the corridors, he felt steps that followed him from behind. Light, feathery, cotton steps. He turned and saw one of the sick children who was walking after him. He recognized him in the twilight. He was a child without anyone in the world. Fernando recognized his face, already branded by death, and those open eyes that seemed to apologize or beg for pardon. Fernando drew close to him, and the child touched him lightly with his hand. "Please, tell . . ." whispered the child, "tell someone that I am here." *

The child is sick, is close to death, and, worst of all, he is alone. Totally alone. And it is Christmas Eve, and he knows it. He senses the first shadows as they begin to close in on the sacred night. He hears the last footsteps on the corridor, and he comes out with the hope of finding company in the nostalgic feast. He is shy and delicate, and will not impose his need on anyone. Only a gentle touch, a low whisper, an innocent plea. Kindly give word, inform, just tell . . . But whom to tell? There is no name in his mind, no relative in his life, no support in his loneliness. So please . . . tell someone. No matter whom. No matter where. Just tell someone I am here. People still have hearts, and someone will come. They will not let a sick child alone on Christmas Eve. Alone with death on his face. Alone in the white corridor of the hospital for children. Alone while the festive rockets burst in the sky. The child is sick, and the name of his sickness is loneliness. The sickness of humankind.

We are moved when we see loneliness in others, and this feeling may help us to fight loneliness in ourselves, and not to cover it up under disguise of a strong character and a stout endurance. Some boast of their capacity to live alone, to stand by themselves, to be independent, to be free from the need of com-

* Eduardo Galeano, *El libro de los abrazos*, p. 172

fort or company or help. They may even see in such an attitude manliness, as they say, and inner strength. Often it is just the opposite. Real strength is needed not to stand alone, but to go out to others, to open up before outsiders, to trust strangers, to venture into dialogue and friendship and love. Loneliness is weakness. And it shows its emptiness in the end by collapsing into itself in barren and rigid isolation.

A merchant in Arab lands used to travel from oasis to oasis on his camel, selling his wares to those who would buy them, and accepting in exchange their food, but rejecting their company. He said that his thoughts and his camel were enough for him, and with his thoughts and his camel he went from place to place, always alone and always apparently satisfied in his self-contained life. One day he chose a lonely spot for his night rest under the open sky, and lay down to sleep without a care on his soul as he considered himself without a need in his body. In the morning, however, when he woke up, he found that his camel had quietly walked out on him and had abandoned him. The camel was wiser than its master. And Arab storytellers do have an instructive sense of humor.

The Dance of the Porcupines

The interplay of the opposite poles of loneliness and intimacy in men's and women's lives is a manifestation of the love-hate polarity in the human heart. The loner hates humankind, and shows his repulsion in his flight from fellow human beings. The lover, on the contrary, draws close and values the direct contact with minds and hearts in familiar exchange. Love and hate are shown in the distances they draw between people who are meant to live together, but can choose to do so either in external appearance only, or in true and genuine companionship. Affective distances define characters.

In a more subtle way, similar distances exist and have influence in all relationships, fixing the degree of closeness, and signaling, with their observable changes, the advances and rejections, the crises and climaxes, attendant on any type of personal dealings. Moods and tempers vary, and when it is not only one individual but two and their mutual relationship that come into play, they shorten and lengthen the distance between souls in a bewitching and bewildering ballet of deep beauty and lovely confusion. The affective distance between two persons is never the same, and its daily and hourly and instant variations constitute the bliss and the blight of the deepest emotion on earth, which is love. A sense of distance is perhaps the most necessary and the most ignored skill in the art of living in society.

Today a companion—perhaps even your spouse—is not in a good mood. Do not inflict on that person your ebullient geniality. Spare them. In order to do so, first notice that they are not up to par just now. Maybe with reason or maybe without it, but they are not right now on your wavelength, and if you blindly insist in bringing them up to your exalted feelings, you will only succeed in alienating them, spoiling a meeting, or starting a quarrel. Wait. Feel your way. Learn how to read faces, to interpret looks, to measure distances. There are moments for a lively talk, and moments for a thoughtful silence. There are occasions for boisterous laughter, and occasions for restrained conversation. There is intimacy and there is reserve. There are times to come closer, and times to keep far. And the discerning spirit is the best friend and the dearest companion. Observance of distance is an essential condition for growth in friendship.

Schopenhauer proposed the celebrated parable of the porcupines in the cold.

> On a freezing winter day, the porcupines in a close herd pressed against each other to warm up with the mutual contact. When doing so, however, they hurt one another with their pointed quills, and they had to separate. The cold drew them together again, and again they pricked each other and fell apart again. The recurring wave of coming

> close and breaking up went on for a while, till they found a
> mean distance in which both evils were alleviated. *

Trial and error. Hurt and relief. Cold and stabs. Warmth and
company. The clumsy movements of the pack of porcupines,
figure and image of the evolutions of men and women in the
winter of life. We feel cold and draw close together by mutual
need. But we are full of quills and thorns and sharp points and
razor edges, and we soon cause each other uneasiness, discomfort, and pain. We are insensitive, thoughtless, boring, and rude.
We impose on others, we criticize, we annoy, we provoke. And
maybe we do not realize that we do it, but we do feel that others
do it to us, and partly to avoid the hurt and partly to teach a lesson
to those who hurt us, we withdraw from their company and
declare that we can live alone in haughty aloofness. But this does
not last long. The chill of loneliness freezes our bones, and we
seek again company in reluctant repentance. We do not come so
close this time. We do not trust people. We keep a careful watch
on the tips of their quills. And the game goes on. The uneasy
crowd heaves and pants, waves and shivers, unites and parts, till
an ephemeral equilibrium is reached, and men and women can
claim that they live in a civilized society. In fact, we are only
playing the game of the porcupines.

Freud, who quotes Schopenhauer's parable, comments further
on it:

> Psychoanalysis reveals that almost all affective relationships
> of any standing between two persons—marriage, friendship,
> parental and filial love—leave as a residue a burden of
> hostile feelings, which can be got rid of only by a process of
> repression. This phenomenon shows itself clearly when we

* Arthur Schopenhauer, in *Parerga und Paralipomena*, second part, *Gleichnisse und
Parabeln*.

see two partners fighting constantly, or a subject forever complaining against his superior. When the hostility is directed against beloved persons, we call it affective ambiguity, and explain it away through the many pretexts that intimate relationships can offer when it is a question of making interests bend toward hatred and violence which makes them into basic human feelings. *

Shortly after I read Freud's book, I happened to watch the famous film *The Postman Always Rings Twice,* and I was amused to see on the screen the vivid representation of what the psychologist had described in his study. Cora and Frank, heroine and hero in the gripping movie, are one moment kissing each other with heartfelt sincerity, and the next moment they are secretly plotting to murder each other with the same heartfelt sincerity. And back to the kissing and back to the plotting till the picture ends in an unexpected climax. The dance of the porcupines in a *pas de deux* of artistic and pathetic realism.

There was another point, however, that especially drew my attention in Freud's text. That was his reference to subjects' complaints against their superiors as expression of a love-hate relationship. In business, politics, family, or religious life, those who are on top know very well that they are the butt of constant criticism, gossip, disguised or manifest opposition. To be under someone, however worthy that person may be and excellent his or her administration, engenders resentment, and the sharpness of many eyes will soon discover the chinks in the boss's personality, and the wit of many tongues will make fun of the public figure, however exalted. Of a certain religious superior, of no mean intellect and natural goodness, it was repeatedly said that he was the greatest bond of union among his subjects in a wide territory, inasmuch as these, however different and opposed in

* Sigmund Freud, *Massenpsychologie und Ich-Analyse,* p. 39.

views and works, were unanimous in criticizing their common superior. I have a suspicion that complaints of religious people against their usually competent and well-meaning superiors can be an unconscious disguise of their inner revolt against God, which they do not dare to express directly, and so deflect toward those who for them represent God on earth. And patient superiors take gallantly the verbal onslaught as part of their job to protect God's image before his chosen people, taking upon themselves the grievances of the suffering faithful. I plan to look into this situation of love-hate relationship with God in a later chapter, when we are better prepared to face ourselves as we are and profit by the consideration.

The dance of the porcupines is not once and for all. With every group and with every person, distance changes from moment to moment, and constant adjustments are required to keep the warmth while avoiding the hurt. Failure to do this can wreck a relationship for a time or forever. There is no greater mistake in friendship than to fix the degree of intimacy with a friend, and come to each encounter with the same measure. The porcupine's quills are sure to stand on edge and do their prickly job.

The wife of a man of high standing, who honored me with his friendship, died, and as soon as I heard the news, I hurried to his home and offered my condolences. He was gracious enough to receive me and sit for a while with me in his suddenly desolate and poignantly empty home. I was eager to show my concern and my fellow feeling, and I spoke. That was a mistake.

In India condolence visits take place in silence. The visitor comes, sits, remains silent for a discreet while, bows deeply, and withdraws. No words are spoken when no words avail. I knew the rubric, but in my keenness to share grief, I overlooked it and spoke of the wonderful woman who had been the soul of that home with her smiling presence, her unfailing service, her ready hospitality, her long, patient, secret suffering of a grievous illness that doctors declared must have caused untold pain which she never allowed anyone to guess. I spoke so much that the bereaved husband was led to respond, and he, too, spoke, describing to me with broken accents the last hours of the woman who had been his very life till a moment too close to recall without rending open the recent wound. We fell silent, but I stayed on. Other people came and went, but I stayed, not finding in my dullness the moment to leave. I was the only one left, and still sat dumbly in the room heavy with grief. It was dark when I finally stood up, bowed, and left. And I sensed that my leaving had brought relief. I had overstayed my visit. I had trespassed on intimacy. I had betrayed friendship. I carried away with me the contrite feeling of emotional guilt. I had damaged a friendship I greatly valued. He never told me anything about this, of course, but my distress was with me. I have carried the memory with me through the years, and it has come up now as a pointed example of a misjudged distance. That day I came too close and hurt a friend. I should have known better.

On another occasion I was bedridden with a sudden sickness. A friend of mine was staying across the road, and I sent word to him, sure that he would lose no time and come at once. He did not show up. The days passed for me, long in the solitude of the white sheets; and no sign of my friend. I assumed he was out of town and could not come. When I was already convalescing and on my feet, he suddenly turned up one day, smiling broadly and holding in each hand an ice cream cone of the variety he knew I fancied. He had been across the road all along, had got my message and knew of my plight, but somehow he had delayed his visit. I was by then strong enough to react, and proceeded to blow my top forthwith. Was that the way to treat a friend? He knew my need, had received my request, and had slept on it. Other people, far less close to me than he was, had visited me those days, some of them even daily, and some coming from out of town, while he had ignored me. If a friend disappears in time of need, what use is his friendship? If he could not cross the road to come and visit me in bed, how could I trust his feelings for me anymore? I was hurt, and let him know it in no uncertain terms.

He reflected with me on his behavior, and came to the conclusion that he had given so much importance to his freedom in his relationship with me that he had for the time being become heedless of my need. He did not want to feel obliged to come, and in that he was right, and I saw and conceded his point, as freedom is essential to a true friendship; but to assert his freedom, he had delayed his coming beyond all reckoning till my sickness was over, and in doing that, he had stretched too far the limits of any meaningful relationship. He had kept too much distance when the circumstances and my explicit request called for closeness. I wryly suggested that when I am at last on my deathbed, he could delay his visit till my funeral to show his freedom. I can be caustic when I choose.

When the exchange was finally over, the ice cream had melted in his hands, though it still looked appetizing. He offered it to me, but I refused to take it. Maybe that was rude of me, but that was how the incident ended, and I do not want to smooth it out in the telling. The fact is that this visit, too, remained in my memory, and has surfaced now when I think of the role distance plays in friendship and love. I only add that the sharpness of my reaction revealed how much I valued that man's friendship, as I would not have taken the trouble to react with such vehemence if I had not cared for him. The point did become clear to me and to my friend, and our bonds were strengthened by the incident. That was well worth missing a favorite ice cream.

It is a law of physics. If the satellite's orbit is too close to the earth, it will fast lose height and be burned in the atmosphere or crash on the surface; and if it is too high, it will fly at a tangent and be lost forever in the endless sky. We are satellites of each other, revolving around and around in the subtle geometry of the celestial spheres. And even the orbits of the planets are elliptical; sometimes far and sometimes close, but never at the same distance. They know their laws and sense their moods, and recede and approach according to seasons and weight and speed, and the heavens stand in the ever-changing and ever steady relationship of its myriad constellations. Cosmic wisdom that we could well bring to bear on our own private astronomy.

A saying of American Indians: "Keep a river between you and a herd of bisons; and keep a boat to cross the river." The bisons are danger and have to be kept at bay beyond the safety of the running waters; but the bisons may be necessary game for food and clothing, and a boat must be at hand for the necessary approach. We all need the river and the boat, the saving distance and the instant contact. And the instinct to know when to hide and when to appear. Persons also can be threatening danger and welcome company. And the seasoned Indian knows the right time for each attitude.

For many years, till urban needs brought buildings and roads to our then open neighborhood, a large and shallow pond of rainwater spread throughout the monsoon months just below the window of my room. It was a favorite haunt for water buffaloes, which loitered in the grass and wallowed in the mud with the leisurely zest for nature's earthly pleasures that characterizes the peaceful animals. I often observed the striking symbiosis between two unlikely partners: the omnipresent black crow of the Indian scene, and the huge reclining buffalo unmindful of the world around it. The bold crow alights fearlessly on the buffalo's back and stays on it unmolested for as long as it pleases. The buffalo does not seem to mind. In fact, there is a secret partnership between both. The crow picks on the insects that have made their home on the generous backside of the patient ruminant, rids its ears of unwelcome guests, and preens the luscious skin of its foppish client. In exchange, the crow gets a varied meal of dainty dishes in an exclusive setting. No wonder the mutual business thrives, and crows on buffaloes' backs are a common sight on the Indian countryside.

The snag comes when the crow stays too long on the buffalo's back. The buffalo is a patient beast, but sometimes it, too, gets tired of so much pecking and probing and jumping and scratching, and it seems to prefer to be left with some insects rather than to bear for long with the officious inquisitiveness of the hungry crow. The buffalo will not resort to violence to drive away its meddlesome partner, but it has a way to signal the limit of its patience, and I watched the repeated scene from my vantage point. The fed-up buffalo rose gently on its four legs, and slowly entered the muddy waters with the crow still on its back. It advanced steadily toward the center of the pool, and the waters lapped its sides and rose imperceptibly. When it reached the spot it knew well for depth and smoothness, it bent first its forelegs and then its hind legs so that its whole body disappeared under the water. The water is not a friendly element for the crow, and so as soon as the tide rose, the reluctant crow beat its wings and took flight. The meal was over for the day, and the buffalo was left in peace with almost a human smile of contentedness on its snout above the waters. A flawless performance.

A wise crow knows when to come and when to leave. It does not wait for the waters to rise. If it wants to preserve the partnership, it should sense in time its partner's moods. In fact, they say that it is always the same crow that pairs with the same buffalo, though I had no means to verify that. To me all crows look alike. And so do all buffaloes for that matter.

Do You Look At Me?

Communication is the soul of relationship. And it is becoming a forgotten art in an age when the communications media are teaching us how not to communicate. *Communication* has become a technical word, and in the process it has lost its content, its meaning, its life. The Indian languages offer a wide choice of words to deal with the fact and experience of personal and social communication, but when a neologism was needed for modern professional use, the experts coined a new word: *pratyayan.* I asked several people in the university staff room what the word meant, and no one was able to give me an answer. I commented, "To say 'communication,' they have chosen a word that does not communicate." The word has even become the title of a new monthly magazine on the subject. I wonder how many subscribers the magazine has.

Think of the following daily occurrence at almost every home. Open the mailbox and examine the contents the postman has left there for the day. There are advertisements, notices, bank correspondence, catalogs, government information, municipality news, sundry papers, and rarely a personal letter, a private message, an intimate communication. We are flooded by a deluge of print, with lovely colors and attractive types, but without a heart in it, and we suffer from the dryness of the printed word that reaches us in merciless onslaught. Gone is the love letter, the long correspondence between friends, the carefully penned missive, the thoughtful answer for the correspondent and for posterity. Every literature used to boast of volumes of printed letters from great men and women whose ideas, elegance, style, and literary taste made even their private correspondence into works of art that deserved and obtained public recognition. Soon, if we want to print the private messages of any public figure, all that will be available to us will be his or her personal computer's printouts, and the recorded tapes from their dictaphones. Hardly a legacy worthy of posterity.

The telephone call is taking the place of the written letter. And, increasingly, the automatic answering machine is taking the place of the telephone. I know of few more frustrating experiences than dialing a number expecting a friendly voice to come up at the other end, only to realize at the first words that a machine is answering me. This is a recording. You can speak your message if you so desire after you hear three beeps. Yes, and you can smash the phone if you so desire in protest and anger at the nonexistent speaker. The machine will not mind. It will go on repeating the frozen message as many times as you work it, with the same words and in the same tone. But there is no present contact, no live dialogue, no meeting of two people, even if only by voice over the wire. A leisurely speaker will or will not answer me at a later time when the urgency of my words has died out and the eagerness of my mind has subsided. My only defense will be to set up an answering machine in my own home to take revenge on the person whom I had called, when he or she calls back. They may leave their message after they hear three beeps. Dialogue by installments. Absence of communication through a device programmed to foster it. Contact without meeting. A link that breaks up ties.

In certain advanced cities there is a "Call a Friend" telephone service in which, by dialing an easily remembered number, one can hear a friendly voice offering kindly advice. The irony is that usually the words one hears in the phone are only a recorded message. The tone is intimate, to be sure, the words are chosen, the ideas are lofty. But there is no person at the other end of the line. There is only a spool turning around and around in a plastic contraption. And they call that a "friend." "Call a Plastic Tape" would hardly be an attractive name for the well-meant program.

Once I offered my services for spiritual counseling to a religious sister who was going to make her annual "retreat," that is, eight days of silence and prayer under someone's direction in a group or individually, as was the case with her. She politely refused, and gave as a reason that she had been fortunate in obtaining the tapes of a retreat preached by a director she appreciated very much, and intended to use them for her spiritual endeavor. I felt slighted, not only because another had been preferred to me, but because I had been given up in favor of a set of tapes. Plastic again, while I am a person and very much alive. Yet she preferred the amateurishly recorded talks for a general public, rather than conversing heart to heart with me. If she liked the tapes so much, she could possibly have kept them for the next year, as plastic is rather durable and would not spoil in that time, while I certainly would not be available again. But she stuck to her choice and went into her prayer experience under the guidance of the machine. There was, of course, a hidden reason behind her choice, which I did not fail to notice. She was afraid of me. She was rather conservative in her ways, and feared that if she revised her spiritual life with me, she would find herself challenged in more than one point and invited to open and to change, and this she wanted to avoid. She was fully within her rights in doing so, and she chose the safety of the recorded tape rather than the adventure of a live encounter. Machines do not answer back.

As machines replace persons, our occasions for communication in daily life diminish, and hours and days can pass without our really meeting anyone in human relationship. Shopping formerly was a social event. The shopkeeper knew us by name, greeted us warmly when we entered, asked us about our families, supplied us with all the gossip in town while willingly listening to whatever rumors we could contribute on our part, and greeted us again when we left. Now the self-service rules supreme. Fast, neat, efficient. Push your cart, take your pick, show your load, listen to the ticks of the bar-code laser counter, check the last figure in the bill, hand in the cash, and move on. The next buyer is already at the counter. Nobody knows you, and you know nobody. A week's purchases without a human meeting. We can get money, gas, a can of beer or a pack of cigarettes, without meeting a person or speaking a word. Machines do the job. We are already learning to move in a robot's universe where life will be impersonal, and communication nonexistent. Science-fiction pictures provide robots with funny-sounding voices to distinguish them from us, the real humans. And I have heard children at play acting as robots and speaking with a hollow voice and jumpy grammar to imitate their mechanical counterparts, thus being almost a prophecy in action of what men and women are destined to be in a not very remote future. Polite machines with mechanical voices in a sterilized world. A dehumanized society.

Eduardo Galeano has another telling anecdote: "Rosa María

Mateo, one of the most popular figures in Spanish television, told me this. A woman from a small remote village had written her a letter asking her please to answer truthfully: 'When I look at you, do you look at me?' Rosa María told me the story, and she said she had not known what to answer" (p. 142). The story is pathetic in its simplicity. And the fallacy in it shows. The woman says, "When I look at you," but, in fact, she is doing nothing of the kind. When the dear old lady in the village is watching Rosa María's show on TV, she is not looking at Rosa María, she is looking at a slightly arched, almost rectangular piece of glass and at the shapes and colors that are projected on it from behind. The woman in the village is not looking at the TV announcer, and the TV announcer cannot look at the woman in the village. It is only an illusion, and the whole immense television business worldwide thrives on it. Good professionals of the little screen act so well, speak so convincingly, look so charmingly into the eye of the camera, which in transmission becomes the eye of the viewer, that even if the program is aired several days later, they seem to be actually talking, conversing, interacting with the candid fans for whom their voices and faces and gestures have become as familiar as those of close friends.

In the loneliness of the remote village, the old woman, who probably lives alone or with little company, sits for hours before the TV set, fills with its color and sound the empty spaces of her retired life, and looks forward with eager anticipation to the regular appearance on the screen of the favorite star with her winning smile, her expressive face, her velvet voice, her telling gestures. And when she appears at the expected time, it is almost as though a meeting took place, and the woman in her home looks at the performing star with wide eyes and warm feelings. Only a little doubt remains in her innocent soul: Does she look at me when I look at her? It does seem so, but she does not know for sure, and it is important for her to know. So she writes a letter, and the very fact of having to write a letter to ask whether she is looking at her should tell her that she is not looking. But the letter goes, and in it a special word to insist that it has to be answered "truthfully." Empty formulae will not do for the wearingly suspicious villager.

Then the TV star receives the letter, is moved by it, and ponders what to answer. The snag is the word "truthfully." She could, in her resourceful ways, write a roundabout answer, or even take the letter to her next TV program, read it there, and assure the faithful watcher that of course she was looking at her right then, didn't she notice it? Beautiful, to be sure, but not quite truthful. Or she could forget the letter. No, she couldn't. The letter questioned her job and challenged her sincerity. She had to unburden herself before a trusted friend. And he, too, was touched, and passed on the story. It opens our eyes to the weakness of modern entertainment. They say that TV is company. Electronic company.

One thing I love TV for is its classical music concerts. For the music lover, it is a supreme treat to be able to hear and to see, even if it is on a small screen, the best orchestras of the world when, conducted by the greatest figures of the baton and the podium, they interpret the masterpieces of the universal repertoire with unfailing perfection. These are moments when I bless humankind's ingenuity and science's inventions and the TV box in its undisputed corner. To bring music to every home is a noble blessing which may well redeem less laudable influences in the little screen business.

On one occasion the work I was getting ready to enjoy on TV was none other than Mozart's Serenade in B-flat, "Gran Partita," of which Johann Friedrich Shink had said when it was first performed in 1784 that it was "glorious and grand, excellent and

sublime"; and which Albert Einstein later called "an extraordi-
nary work that is far above all earthy standards and borders on the
immaterial." I had lowered myself deep into my armchair, had
adjusted the controls, and was looking forward to an uninterrupted spell of paradise. And so at the beginning it seemed it
would be. But something went wrong. The musicians were excellent, the conductor full of feeling and expression, and the
music perfect. But as the performance advanced, I noticed that
the concert had been recorded in an empty theater. It was a large
hall, with row upon row of comfortable seats, the high boxes, the
large gallery, but not a soul in them. And the music sounded
hollow. I wanted to have faces to see my joy reflected in them,
my bliss multiplied in their expressions. But there were only
empty seats and carpeted floors. Something was missing. The
audience. The human presence. The ovation at the end. Sometimes we sing alone in life to an empty hall. And we miss the fun.

The art of conversation is a dying art. The after-dinner chat,
the informal gathering, the leisurely exchange, the deep and
witty give and take of ideas between intellectual friends who love
to think and to see how others think in the noble exercise of
humans' highest faculty. There is no time for that in our busy
schedules. We are headed for a formal business meeting which is
to begin at an exact time, with a fixed agenda, a standard procedure, and a time limit. No small talk there. Neither at our
office with the daily pressure of work, the meetings, interviews,
decisions, dictation. Then the time spent in going to and coming
from work in the lonely impatience of the private car or the
crowded solitude of public transport. Perhaps time to read a novel
or listen to the radio through discreet headphones. But no time
to talk. Home is restful, but our mind is tired, the faces too
familiar and life too dull for earnest conversation. A few kind
words, light family gossip, perhaps plans for tomorrow, and

switching on TV again if it was not already on during dinner. No time for dialogue.

I know few greater pleasures on earth than heart-to-heart conversation with friends. Heart to heart and mind to mind. From playful fooling to serious disquisition, and from commenting on personal news to setting right the affairs of the whole world. Ideas jump up in the mind one on top of the other, hardly allowing time for one another in the wild excitement of congenial speculation. New thoughts flash, unexpected and different views thrive, rabidly challenged or enthusiastically welcome. Feeling helps thought, and language itself flowers in the sudden spring of the intense encounter and the relaxed intimacy. And time is forgotten while two souls unite in the light and warmth of common ideas and shared feelings. Communication is what brings us close to other human beings, and this closeness is the very heart and secret of personhood. We are persons insofar as we relate, in thought and affection, to other persons who in turn are shaped and enriched by their meeting us. That is why there is joy in communication and pleasure in dialogue. We grow by contact, and the deeper the contact, the greater the growth. Strange that we do not find time in our lives for this quiet, intimate, genuine, quickening contact. Or maybe in our heart of hearts we do not want to grow, perpetual Peter Pans of safe and easy childhood.

Yet, in our true selves, we do want to be contacted. We want to be noticed, to be called, to be wanted. We know that our salvation is in the midst of our fellow human beings, and we long for their company and strive for their attention. "Love me or hate me, but for heaven's sake, do not ignore me" is the cry of the human heart, sometimes in spite of itself, but always as a real need for breath and life. To be ignored is to die. And the way not to be ignored is not to ignore others. We ignore others when we go through our day without looking at people, without talking with them, without stopping to chat, without paying attention, without showing interest, without opening ourselves to them so that they in turn may open up to us and we may establish the bonds that make us human. To ignore people is to treat them as things, as material objects, as machines that have no feelings and no personality. To ignore people is to miss life, to drive oneself into exile, to insult humankind, to court loneliness. To ignore people as we live among them is to be blind in a world of light. Self-imposed punishment of dreary dejection.

Communication is, of course, more than words. A look, a smile, a handshake, a caress. Senses that speak affection, and gestures that show concern. Whatever expresses to the other person that we have taken notice, that we appreciate, that we care. Or simply that we are present, with conscious awareness of our own stand here and of the nearness and existence of other people around, and form a grateful and joyful part of this group that at the moment is experiencing life together. If I am alive to the fact that other men and women are just now here, that inner consciousness will show by itself and send its coded messages and elicit responses and awaken feelings and make us feel at home in the common task of living like a family on earth. Let us learn how to make our presence felt, not in the sense of wielding influence and exerting pressure, but in the quite different sense of bringing life to a meeting and joy to a group. If we are truly alive, our very presence will light the air and sharpen the sounds and shorten distances and create an atmosphere where people will feel friendly and approach one another with grace and attention. It is our role to bring friendliness into the world by being friendly ourselves. That is our best contribution to the building of a happier society.

A woman who was in the habit of giving alms to a beggar at the door of the church reached one day for her purse, only to realize that she had forgotten to bring it with her. The beggar's hand was still extended toward her when she reacted tactfully and said, "I have nothing with me to give you today, but I can at least shake your hand." And she did so with a graceful, heartfelt gesture. The beggar rose to the occasion, yielded to the handshake, and said, "Today you gave me more than any other day." The human touch is the most precious gift we can bring to the life of those around us.

Safety on the Road

When I arrived in India, an old missionary who had lived in the country many years after coming from abroad, and had never succeeded in learning properly the language of the land, quoted his experience to me and gave me his advice. He had thought, he said, though mistakenly, as facts would show in time, that he would learn his second language as he had learned the first, that is, simply by being there, by osmosis, by inertia, without grammar lessons or spelling practice. He had learned his mother tongue without knowing he was learning it, and was sure that the process would repeat itself after thirty years in another land. But it did not. The language he learned was faulty, and his pronunciation remained foreign. When he tried to improve his practice, it was too late, and he never obtained a satisfactory knowledge of the language. He was a shy man, and he suffered till the end of his long life from the handicap that prevented him from easily and freely meeting others and leading a full social life. His advice was: Do not take things for granted; skills are not learned by themselves; make the effort soon and master the art before it is too late.

Communication is an art and has to be learned. We need practice, observation, reflection, mistakes, correction, planning, effort, daily improvement, and lifelong perseverance. It does not come by itself. On the contrary, the more time elapses, the greater the difficulty in mastering accents in pronunciation and idioms in grammar. We think too lightly of conversation, meetings, dialogue. We seem to know what to do; we know how to speak and how to answer a question and how to join a discussion. It is all easy and simple and taken for granted. And the years pass and the vocal cords harden and the voice sets and behavior settles, and one day we realize that we are too stiff and withdrawn and lonely and aloof, and then it may seem too late to learn new songs and dance new steps. We want to come closer to people, but our image precedes us and bars the way to intimacy. Our voice does not invite, our face is dull, our manners are frozen, our feelings are out of practice, and we cannot anymore be what we would like to be, what we had all along dreamed we could be in geniality of character and charm in conversation. All that is left for us is to resign ourselves to flatness, or perhaps to justify with the logic of regret the affective sterility in which we are trapped.

Before that happens, it will be well for us to wake up and take notice. If our mind is stirred while thinking of these things and reviewing our life and projecting our dreams, this means that we are still alive and can become even more so if we sharpen ideas and risk experience. The classroom is open, and we walk into it every day, if only we know now how to profit from encounters and meetings, from a passing greeting and a quiet talk. People are all around us, and we all are students and teachers in the wide laboratory of human relations. We can help ourselves by thinking about the importance of relationships and the means to improve communication, which is the practical way to relate to others.

We are poor communicators. There is hardly a proportion between the amount of words we speak and the amount of information we convey. And there is no end to the confusion between what we think we have conveyed and what the other person in fact experiences as conveyed to him or her. Since we usually do not take the trouble to check whether what we meant is what has been understood, we expose ourselves to constant misunderstandings and the consequent mishaps. Once a kind friend presented our kitchen with a choice piece of fresh country ham, and instructed the cook how to prepare it to full taste and best advantage. The cook nodded understanding and went to work. He was a fine lad with a sense for spices and sauces, but he had never seen country ham in his life. He had been told to cut it in thin slices, which he did, but then he boiled the tiny bits out of recognition and destroyed all the fine taste in them. We had anticipated a good meal, and were horrified when the dish arrived on the table with the unrecognizable ham in a tasteless stew. The cook was summoned, and he assured us he had followed instructions to the letter. To the letter, that is, as understood by him, which was something quite different from what had been intended by the expert who had presented the ham and had given the instructions. Failure in communication resulted in a spoiled meal.

Carl Rogers recommends a simple practice to improve our performance in communication, and, more than that, to make us realize the need to improve it. When any dialogue, discussion, encounter, is in progress and we are freely taking part in it, proposing our ideas and commenting on those of others, we are just directed to summarize what a person has said before responding to it. Someone, say, has expressed an opinion, and I want to take exception to it. I can surely do so, but before I manifest my opposition, I am instructed to repeat briefly what he or she has said, and to check whether my summary does justice to their thought, and only then can I proceed to express my own opinion. More often than not we find in such an exercise that our perception of the other person's point of view had not been entirely accurate, and in the exchange that follows, to refine my understanding of the other's position before I expose my own, I may find that my perception of what has been said changes substantially, and no differences in fact remain.

This may look like a lengthy process, and people engaged in brisk dialogue may feel irritated if each time they want to butt in, they have first to offer an official résumé of what the other person has said; but if the conversation lasts long enough, it will be found that this roundabout way is actually a shortcut, because eventually it does away with the otherwise unavoidable protests like "That is not what I said," "You have misunderstood me," "Let me say it again." Without such clarifications, the same thing has to be repeated indeed again and again till it conforms to the original statement. By the time it does, we begin to see how difficult it is to reproduce what someone else has said, how we at once rush into our own interpretation of it, how we do not even allow the other person to finish and we give a rejoinder before the case has been exposed, and a friendly discussion can be transformed into a verbal free-for-all where all talk and nobody listens.

It pays to speak clearly, to repeat the essence of the message, and to make sure that it has been properly understood. Often we are obscure, ambiguous, fragmentary. We are vague, blurred, and imprecise; at times we are also prolix, long-winded and repetitious, and the repetitions do not clarify the issue but make it more confused, as no statement exactly corresponds to a previous one. We take for granted that the other person knows what we want to say, and the assumption is a very dangerous one. In most cases the other person does not know, at least not with the nuances and details the subject has with us now, and to presume that, because we have just mentioned the issue, it must immediately show in our partner's mind as it shows in our own mind is unwarranted, overoptimistic, and rash. We can never be too clear.

Aaron T. Beck comments aptly on this point in his book *Love Is Never Enough:*

> It is distressing to observe how poorly some otherwise articulate people fare when it comes to communicating their thoughts, desires, and feelings with their own partners. Some state their wishes in a way that defies understanding. They express their opinions vaguely, talk around the point, get lost in trivial details—all under the bland assumption that their partner grasps what they are trying to say. One partner may swamp the discussion with excessive verbiage while the other impoverishes it with a paucity of words— both erroneously believing that they are contributing to mutual understanding. Sometimes, they seem to be speaking different languages; they use the same words, but the message sent is totally different from the message received. It is not surprising, given such faulty communication styles, that both partners feel frustrated. Since each is oblivious to his or her own contribution to the murky exchange, blame is laid at the other mate for being obtuse or bullheaded. Marjorie, for example, wanted Ken to invite her to a favorite cocktail lounge overlooking a bay to celebrate their anniversary. She archly asked him, "Ken, do you feel like going out for a drink tonight?" Ken, who was feeling tired, missed the hidden message contained in her question. He responded, "No, I'm too tired." Marjorie was extremely disappointed. Only after feeling hurt and sorry for herself did she realize that she had not communicated to Ken her real desire—to celebrate their anniversary.

When she later made clear her true wish, he readily agreed
to celebrate. *

Perfect non-dialogue. "Do you feel like going out tonight?"
"No." The real reason has not been communicated, and so the
expected reaction does not take place. And then comes recrim-
ination and hurt and sulking. "He should have known. Wasn't it
our wedding anniversary? Do I have to spell out every word?"
And on the other side: "How could I know? Can't she call things
by their names? Do I have to guess what she really means every
time?" Things would have been much simpler for both if the real
desire had been stated from the beginning with neat clarity and
candid request. "Today is our wedding anniversary, and I would
love to celebrate it with you at that place you and I know so well."
That is a perfect starter, and negotiations can take place on it.
Fear, shyness, pride, hesitancy, can keep us from taking the
straight approach in order not to risk a refusal or a criticism. That
is precisely why clarity in expression is important: It shows that
we are also clear on the inside and courageous in stating our
desires. If we truly know what we want and say it gently, we shall
be surprised at the number of times we get it without problems.

Stereotypes are poor communication. And yet our speech is
loaded with them, with the best of intentions and the worst of
results. "What can I do for you?" I am not quite sure what you
can do for me, but just now by asking me that trite question, you
are making me feel I am in a shop and you are the shopkeeper,
which is not a very helpful thought in my present situation, and
so maybe the best thing you can do right now for me is to shut up
and not utter platitudes. "I know how you feel, because I went
through something very similar myself." Unfortunately, I should

* Aaron T. Beck, "Static in Communication," in *Love Is Never Enough* (New York:
Harper & Row, 1989), p. 91.

say, as now you have taken my story only as an excuse to present your own story. You certainly do not know how I feel at this moment, not particularly how I feel about you; and if you knew it, you would make yourself scarce before you come to your next comment. "You know you can always count on me." If at least I could count on you to keep quiet when you have nothing to say, that would be a relief. To purge our language of stereotypes is, apart from healthy linguistics, a good exercise in improving communication.

If I want something to be done, the right way is to present it as my own wish and desire, and not to try to put it onto someone else so that he or she may have the onus of asking and I may get the benefit of the other person's initiative. This is a common trick constantly repeated. Do you want an ice cream? The one who is dying for an ice cream is myself, but I do not want my respectable person to appear interested in such a base product as a vile ice cream, and so I put on a generous mask of concern for my friend who might care for that trifle, and I show myself to be good enough to condescend to his childish whim and even accompany him in his weakness for charity's sake so that he may not feel shy. Quite a show of selfless considerateness on my part. The trouble is that the other person may ignore my solicitude, may not be partial to ice cream and may refuse the offer, leaving me without the cool treat I had thought to be within easy reach. After his refusal, of course, it would not be dignified on my part to confess that I wanted the ice cream anyhow for myself and buy one and take it. Abstinence will prevail and dignity will be upheld.

Once I was in danger of my life as a result of one such twisted transaction. It happened this way. A friend of mine was taking me in his car to a distant place which would take us several hours to reach. We had started right after lunch, and after three hours of continuous driving, we were about halfway to our destination.

At the beginning of the drive and for quite some time we had been engaged in a lively conversation on topics of mutual interest, which, as my friend was a very intelligent and knowledgeable person, had resulted in a most entertaining and enlightening exchange. Now we were both quiet, he intent on his driving, and I admiring the landscape that was taking us through a chain of mountains with thrilling curves and awesome precipices. As a village came into view, my friend broke the silence and proposed, "Would you like a cup of coffee?" I answered instantly, "No. I'm not a coffee drinker and don't feel like any other drink just now. I'd much rather keep on enjoying this wonderful landscape." We passed through the village without stopping, and the driving continued. After a while another village appeared on the horizon, and as we approached it, my friend repeated his offer: "Do you care for a cup of coffee?" I again declined the offer: "No, no. Honestly I don't care for coffee. Thank you very much for your concern for me, but I prefer to go on with our ride." So we did for some more time. Then a third village appeared after a curve on the road, and my friend on seeing it exploded and said with vehemence, "Look here, Carlos. I am driving this damned car for three hours, I am tired and I am literally falling asleep on the wheel, and if I don't have a break and a cup of coffee, we are going to go down the next ravine instead of reaching our destination, if that is what you seem to prefer. Tell me now, do you care for a cup of coffee, yes or no???" I lifted both my arms and shouted desperately, "Yeeees!!! I positively love coffee!!!" He stopped the car in front of a bar, and we went in. We took two cups of coffee each. I am not a coffee drinker, but I must confess that on that occasion the coffee tasted really good. My friend still took a third cup on my selfless and considerate request. Then we went back to the road. Before sunset we safely reached our destination.

The Perfume of the Rose

Faulty communication can cause accidents on the roads of life. And superficial communication keeps life superficial. The level of intimacy we achieve in variety of persons and depth of contact can be a good measure of the strength and worth of our personality. I have by now lived long enough to see how people who in earlier years boasted of a marked individuality that needed no friends and sought no support, declined later in life and even underwent heavy crises in their affective solitude and lofty isolation. To put up a brave front of distance and independence may work for some time, but in the end the front only serves to hide the strain of a lonely life.

When a person comes to me to speak about personal matters, and begins by telling me that I am the first person to whom he or she is revealing that story, I feel unhappy. I know that such a revelation is meant as a compliment to me, but I also realize that if I am the first person to whom it is told, the person must have lived his or her situation in isolation, and that will complicate the problem and delay the answer. The very fact of speaking for the first time shows the strain and the lack of familiarity with the ways of the heart. No practice in opening up, no inclination to talk, no urge to share. That tension itself may be, if not the cause, at least the multiplying factor of the troubles, and in any case will stand in the way when a solution is sought and support needed. The sooner we learn to open up, the better. That is the best way to communicate.

If the heart of relationship is communication, the heart of communication is self-revelation. To open the window, to show one's face, to lift the veil. That is the ultimate communication and the underlying message in all genuine contacts. If I am not in some way in them, my words have no value. Information can be pure gossip, and conversation can be only noise. Unless the person comes through, the most refined speech is empty verbiage, and perfect sentences are mere sound. What gives value to all that I say is ultimately myself, and if I hide myself behind my speech instead of using it to reveal myself, I am misusing language and missing my chance to come out, to make contact, to grow into life.

I was taking part in a sensitivity program with previously unknown people, and one of them proposed that we begin the session by a self-introduction round. We did. After a while, when three or four people in the group had told their life histories, the director of the encounter simply got up and left the room. Later he explained his action, which he had meant as a hint to be interpreted and acted upon by the group. He said that what we had begun to do was the opposite of communication, and it was urgent that we should realize it. We had begun telling our stories, yes, but in a purely objective and impersonal way, and that led nowhere. If there was anything important in our lives, that would surface later in our sessions at its proper time and with its proper depth. Mere narratives were useless. Dates and events and biographies gave an impression that we were saying something, while in fact we were only wasting our time and hindering the communication process by hiding behind our narratives. Facts in themselves are not important; it is only when they are presented as live experiences and shot through with personal feeling and exclusive individuality that they acquire relevance and touch hearts. Facts are only the façade, which can be used simply to be admired from outside, or to enter the building through its door. On that occasion, at the opening session of a group encounter, we had defensively lapsed into impersonality disguised as life histories. We soon learned that such was not the way to interact fruitfully.

A similar story from a Zen master. After much training and not a few discourses, one day he invited his disciples to express themselves in the presence of all the others in any way they wanted, about their experiences in the school. Some exposed their convictions, some told experiences, some asked questions. Their master did not leave the hall, but remained quizzically quiet in typical Oriental pose. Finally a student spoke and said, "My feet are cold." And the master smiled and bowed toward him. The accolade that consecrated his answer as the only valid one. The disciple smiled back and bowed to his master.

The person who says, "My feet are cold" is saying something real, personal, present. It may not be a very transcendental revelation, but it does express, in its humble and earthly matter-of-factness, something that is happening right here in the middle of the whole group, and that bodily affects one of them. There is no need even to see a cryptic criticism of the dullness of his colleagues in the double-meaning expression "cold feet," apart from whether the expression has the two meanings also in the Chinese language, which I do not know. No mystery, no hidden message, no parable. Just a pair of cold feet in a bare room. And the direct and objective mind of the owner of the feet, which notices the fact and expresses it as it is. There is no complaint either in the innocent statement. The master does not ask for the brazier to be lit, or for the cold feet to be massaged. He just smiles and bows. The cold feet remain cold. But the atmosphere in the room is not cold anymore. A spark of reality has changed the routine exchange into a bit of life.

How many meetings, dialogues, discussions, could be enlivened by someone saying at the right moment, "My feet are cold"! That was not, of course, on the agenda, and it will not be recorded in the minutes, but it may be that it was the only sincere thing that was said at the meeting, and would at least bring a smile of earthly contentment to the lips of the members of the board. To be in touch with my feelings, and in this case with my feet, is a sign of sanity and condition of life. And to say what I feel, with liberty and simplicity, is to open a door and to build a bridge. Communication can now take place.

Psychologists use the terms *history* and *narrative* to distinguish these two types of intervention in a group. The terms are rather arbitrary, but they do help to classify the facts and keep concepts apart. A history is an impersonal, objective, detached exposition of one's life or part of it. A narrative is a first-person account, with personal feeling and concrete approach. In practice it is easy to distinguish one from the other. Pure history bores. It is long and can be continued without interruption. Neither the tone nor the words of the speaker invite questions, queries, or comments. The historian almost keeps aloof from his or her history without getting involved in it, and that is why it turns out dull. Nobody is interested in a series of facts. Often such a display of information is precisely the opposite of what it was meant to be; that is, instead of being communication and contact, it becomes a shield and a barrier that prevents real communication. Much is spoken so that nothing may be said. One has fulfilled one's duty to the group or to the individual listener. The story has been told. Now there is a pause. Someone else will come up with another story, and the game will go on. At the end nobody has learned anything about anybody, and all are bored stiff. This happens in group encounters, in social gatherings, and in ordinary conversation, and in all it is equally empty and frustrating. Pure description of facts and events without personal involvement leads nowhere, and it can be harmful insofar as it creates the illusion of communication while it actually hinders it.

True self-revelation is different. The "narrator" is fully in the narrative. There is selection of events, there are pauses, there are looks to scan the surrounding faces for understanding, for queries, for challenge, there is a positive standing invitation to everybody around to take part in the proceedings with freedom and love. Genuine self-revelation on the part of one person invites a corresponding self-revelation from whoever listens with kindred sensitivity. In fact, it facilitates such an exchange at a deep level, by taking the risk first and showing that it can be taken without any dire consequences.

When such a climate of mutual self-revelation is created between two persons or more, there is a kind of magic effect in the air and in the hearts of the participants. We know that we have reached heart level, and that makes all the difference. There is no need for anyone to say it, to point it out, to draw attention to it. We are facing one another person to person, and every word has echoes, and every smile elicits understanding, and we draw closer to each other as we listen and talk and allow the privileged experience to evolve itself with its own rhythm and its own warmth. Is not the opening of a rose its self-revelation? Its perfume reaches all those who can stand close and watch the wonder. That is the way to make a garden out of this world. Open up, and let the perfume spread.

Lifting the Veil

Self-revelation changes both the person who speaks and the person who listens. When I open up before you, be it in a passing confidence or in a long, introverted mood, I am literally being myself before you, and by being myself in your eyes, I am myself in my own eyes too. I see myself expressed in my words and reflected in your face. I know myself better as I struggle to put into words what so far was only speechless experience, I gain perspective as I break the monologue of my own memory, I see my failures and my hits as I guess your silent reaction to my candid unveiling. So I change while I speak of myself before you in trustful communion. And you, too, change when listening to me, as glimpses of another life enlighten your own by contrast or support, as you see the common striving for human excellence in the different while similar circumstances of a life close to yours. I have said earlier that relationships shape us, and this is the choice instrument and the privileged activity through which they do it: self-revelation.

I had known a person for some time in a pleasant but rather superficial kind of relationship. It was nice to meet him, speak with him, listening to his comments on events we both knew, and offering him mine. All in a general, amicably social sort of way. One day, however, without any special reason, but in tune with the silent mood and quiet corner in which we were seated, he grew introspective and began to speak of some more personal matters with tentative sensitivity. He knew he was treading new ground, but he trusted himself, he trusted me, and ventured gently into it. He spoke slowly and kept his eyes down; he then paused and looked up to check my face. By then I had sensed the change of mood and was all attention and respectful expectation. He continued, delving a little deeper at each turn of the verbal spiral. At a point, when he wanted comment, he let it be known by his change of posture and his telling look. I matched his mood with mine, not to impose my own self-revelation on him, which would have destroyed the confidence, but to encourage his with pointed understanding and parallel feeling; and then he continued with inner ease, without ever trespassing on the initial shyness of a first rapprochement. What he said was not very important, and my own comments were far from weighty; but I knew that a door had been opened, that I was invited to come closer and enrich my life with his. Our relationship was never the same after that.

The same thing happens in a group. We may have been together for hours, planning work, evaluating performances, exchanging ideas with the clarity and efficiency of people who know each other and live together and want to think out things and understand situations and help people. And all that is done with the genuine interest of dedicated workers. But sometimes, without planning or expecting, things go further, to the gentle amazement and general profit of all those present. Someone, without any request or provocation, touches thoughtfully on a more personal point. A face is shown, and the group comes alive. The whole atmosphere is changed, pencils are dropped, postures shift, bodies relax, and minds wake up to the sudden gift of a live encounter. A person has walked into the group, and the group changes from discussion to interaction, from past to present, from work to life. That group, too, will never be the same again.

Self-revelation has the power to change past into present. If I tell you now some events of my past life, that is not to relate ancient history or dust my own archives; if I speak of the past, it is insomuch as it is now bearing on my present, and I feel it that way. And so, while telling you about previous happenings, I am uncovering present moods. There is no point in reciting my biodata before you; but there is all the sense in the world in my telling you now how that incident in my childhood has remained in my memory, how it has weighed in my life, and how even today I can see its import, and I heal my soul while I tell the experience. A good test for authentic self-revelation can be the amount of interest it generates in the listener. If the one who listens gets bored, there was no genuine revelation. The facts were only dry facts and were not charged with the live feelings of the present telling. True self-revelation always commands attention and excites interest, because a human person is the most alive thing in the world. If I speak about myself and no one takes notice, I am not truly speaking about myself. My listeners' response is a measure of my sincerity, and a warning if I extend myself beyond limits in length or in prudence. If the link is broken, that means I have fallen into routine reporting. The light in me has dimmed out, and so its reflection in others has become pale too. When the fire is burning, its sparks are bright.

Social dealings are, in fact, so stereotyped and standardized and routinized that a personal touch feels like a whiff of fresh air in the midst of a stifled atmosphere. People will not directly ask for the spell to be broken and for someone to embark on intimate dealings to deepen the exchange, but subconsciously we all often desire that those close to us may come closer and enliven the monotony of life with the warmth of true companionship.

Once a friend presented me on some festive occasion with an artistic letter pad. The meaning of the gift was obvious. She wanted to know more about me. She wanted me to write to her, and as the paper was no ordinary blank stationery, but was very tastefully decorated with a different design on every sheet, it seemed to convey the message that the writing she wanted from me was also no ordinary formal writing of outside news and fixed greetings, but the more personal, and each time different, expression of genuine care and real feelings. As I reflect that I have received letter pads as gifts more than once, I realize that the desire to know more about people may be greater than often assumed. And I have also given letter pads as gifts. I, too, like to know about people.

We all go around in this world with thick veils before our faces. We do not show our true preferences, our real feelings, our opinions, or our reactions. We disguise and dissemble and hide and cover our true image with the hundred masks of formalism and simulation. We do not meet face-to-face but mask-to-mask, and can go through life hardly meeting anybody in truth. We miss the beauty and wealth and wisdom and joy and warmth and love of real persons in real life. And we move away, disappointed and frustrated in our expectations and our hopes. We must recover faces to restore faith in life.

There is one veil we can definitely lift in our lives, and that is our own. Not, of course, at any time and before anybody, but wisely and gently when occasion comes and feelings prompt. Self-revelation by one person is an invitation, discreet and polite, to self-revelation by the others. There is no explicit request, no demand, no pressure, as indeed no outside power can force the unveiling of the soul. But the humble and courageous gesture cannot pass unnoticed in the crowds of men and women who lead similar lives. One veil that is lifted is mirror and parable. If one veil is lifted, so can all the others. The threat is gone and the singularity disappears. The unveiling of a face leads to the unveiling of the others. A moment may arrive when the awkward thing will be to keep the veil once all have removed it. When a climate of mutual trust is created, we can live among men and women instead of the shrouded community of ghosts under the veil. Personal, intimate dealings are the way to bring back to society the life and zest that formalism and rigidity and fear have taken away from it.

We all give gifts to one another on recurring dates in festive calendars. Birthdays and weddings and anniversaries and Christmas and Mother's Day and Father's Day and whatever new day may be invented and launched by a competitive industry that thrives on production and distribution of whatever the market can bear. Behind the business aspect of the gift industry, there is a genuine attitude of love and care, without which the commercial setup could not subsist. The fact is that giving a gift means, in acted parable, giving myself. My gift is part of me, my messenger, my affection, my voice. It can be flowers or jewelry, it can be a book or even plain money, but it goes from me, it takes my place, it says with its unequivocal and permanent language that I am stretching out my hand, I am widening my eyes, I am giving something in pledge because I want to give myself inasfar as I can and circumstances allow me. The only gift I can really give is myself. And every gift parcel that goes from me is part of me in its content, its meaning, its care. I define myself in the gift I choose. My taste, my choice, the type of gift that has to match the personality of the giver as much as that of the receiver, and its value which measures in cold figures my own appreciation of my relationship with the receiver of the gift. All that is carefully packed in the gift box with the colorful wrapping and the golden ribbon. The gift is lovingly packed because my heart goes with it, whatever the material contents of the box may be.

The trouble is that gift giving has become such a routine activity that instead of reminding us of its deep meaning, it blurs it and makes us forget it, as the gift becomes a substitute for the feeling, and it makes us forget the person instead of renewing the personal bond. Birthday remembered, gift sent, person forgotten. Maybe the whole event was only a red mark in a diary and a hint to a secretary to choose and send the gift. There are agencies that can do this on a subscription basis for years in succession, and which undertake not only to send the gift on the exact day, but to remind the sender that the gift has been sent so that he or she may not show surprise when thanked for it. This is a sad devaluation of a beautiful rite.

Every gift, big or small, should, in fact, remind me that in giving it, I am giving myself. And with the reminder should come the desire to convert the material gift into a more intimate one where the soul replaces the object, and the gift takes the form of self-giving in ideas, affection, and life. The ultimate gift that I can make to my friends, to society, to whosoever may know me and follow my life and look at me, is the gift of my self-revelation. More, I cannot give.

Vyas and Ganesh

The topics of our conversation with others can provide an enlightening measure of our closeness or remoteness from them. With a perfect stranger we can comfortably speak of the weather, of politics in general, of the current war, and of the obvious and steady deterioration of moral values and public services in whatever part of the world we may find ourselves at the moment. All that is safe and remote and impersonal. With colleagues we can talk shop. A common field of action offers an unending variety of themes, experiences, events, and criticism to keep the conversation going, to supply and receive information without getting too close, as the office is far from the home. Among friends we can discuss family situations, financial problems, health, and moods, even worries about the future and doubts about eternity. Religion, both in its teachings and in our experience of them, is a fertile field for fruitful contact in mutual trust. To speak to one friend about our relationship to other friends is already a closer approach of special confidence. And perhaps the greatest degree of intimacy is obtained when we speak with a friend about our relationship to him or her. How do we feel about each other, how do we stand with each other, what place do we occupy in each other's life, how do we see the future of our relationship? This is the closest we can come in openness and acceptance.

Lovers do this all the time. Do you love me? Do I love you? Do we love each other? Do you love me more than before? Less than before? Till when will you love me? Will you ever forget me? Do you love anyone else? Did you ever love anyone else? Do you love me more every day that passes as I do love you? In letters or in dialogue this is the constantly recurring and eternally unending theme that underlies every other theme and shows in every word. It can be overdone, of course, and reduction of all topics of conversation to this single one amounts to the reduction of the whole of mankind to a single individual, which may work enthusiastically for a while, but will not last forever; but the readiness to talk with a person about our very relationship to that person is certainly a measure of the degree of closeness we want with him or her. If my relationship with you comes up in my talks with you, that means I care for it and value it. Casual acquaintances do not speak of their bonds.

There is a limit also to closeness and intimacy, and precisely because the gift is precious, it has to be treated with delicacy and respect. Self-revelation can become jarring and defeat its purpose if it is attempted too early, too suddenly, and goes too fast before the other person has time to prepare acceptance and response. I have said that self-revelation invites a corresponding gesture from the person to whom it is directed; and if this person is not ready to correspond at the moment with a parallel revelation, he or she will feel threatened, forced, and imposed upon by the intruding intimacy, and will react with hardness and withdrawal, and will

be fully right in doing so. Whoever trespasses on another's feelings in the name of friendship is not entitled to it and forfeits any
claim to attention. To go about baring one's breast before all and
sundry, at the least provocation and without due preparation, is
no gesture of friendship but a show of insensitivity. Intimacy does
not lie that way. Our self-preservation instinct covers not only
bodily dangers but emotional attacks too, and warns us when
someone gets ready to launch an irresponsible and unauthorized
assault on our privacy. Attackers will be pushed back with determination and efficiency. Only I can issue a visa for my territory.

On the other hand, it would be unwise never to issue visas for
my territory. Shyness is a good protection and, as Socrates said,
"an ornament of virtue"; but it should not become an insur-
mountable barrier. Some social groups, particularly for men,
seem to encourage toughness and relegate intimate confidences
to sentimental weaklings. That apparent toughness is in reality
fear and insecurity. Intimacy takes courage and involves risk, and
we may instinctively recoil from the frightening unknown.

I have noticed that when people approach a personal matter in
conversation, they usually apologize and try to find some sort of
excuse for doing so. "I feel I must tell somebody," "I hope you
don't mind," "Since the point has come up, I can just as well . . ."
"Besides, this could give you matter for an article, only don't
mention my name in it," "Funny, to hear myself speak like this,
and I hadn't quite planned it this way, but since we are at it . . ."
"I know this is going to bore you, but I count on your patience."
There is absolutely no need for an excuse. On the contrary, to
initiate a confidence is the greatest compliment that can be paid
to the listener, and as such should not be preceded by an apology.
But social prejudice, lack of habit, and a hidden streak of shyness
make the formality necessary, and the hesitating words are pronounced and the uneasy smile appears and the halting confession

begins. Doubtful rituals that hinder normal dealings. One has to set people at ease before they start talking about themselves. The most important topic of conversation is the more difficult one to broach.

The greatest danger of self-revelation is not to be accepted. To be ignored, to be brushed aside with an empty gesture, perhaps even to be ridiculed. There are insensitive people who, themselves afraid of affective closeness, protect themselves by rejecting the candidate. This can cause hurt, dejection, frustration. If I open my heart and am laughed at for it, it is going to take me a long time to go and open my heart again. Perhaps I shall never do it anymore. Inner wounds take long to heal. This is the risk I take when I come out and show my face, and I know it. The risk underlines the value of the undertaking. A bold rejection is not likely to take place among sensible people, but a lack of fellow feeling, a polite indifference, a bland paternalism, is more likely to be met with, and it can also do harm. I speak out my soul in search of inner relief and parallel understanding, and I meet with the routine coldness of an insensitive listener. I have drawn a blank. It was not the proper person or the proper moment. At least I can learn how to evaluate persons and to measure moods. A useful art in life.

I can also learn how to be supportive to others when they honor me with their own private stories. To listen without interrupting, without judging, without getting distracted. To listen, but not precisely in order to give advice, not to wait for the other person to stop and then offer my own parallel story to match the other's experience, not even to try to solve the problem or to assuage feelings with unwanted interference. Just to listen. The greatest compliment and the dearest service we can offer a fellow human being. To listen with interest, with affection, with concern. Not to choose when to pay attention and when to let the mind drift while the head keeps bowing in approval with studied hypocrisy. To listen with the whole of me to the whole of you. To listen actively, encouragingly, fraternally. Not to be worried with my own tale while I listen to yours. To live your story with you, and to show it in the keenness of my eyes, in the truth of my expression, in the deepness of my breath. Martin Buber said, "I want to give the total me to the total you," and if speaker and listener can catch a glimpse of that ideal and bring it to life in their exchange, blessed will their friendship be.

One warning. To accept does not mean to approve. More exactly, to accept the person does not mean to approve of all he or she does. To listen encouragingly does not mean to encourage all the other person does, which may conceivably be quite condemnable in itself. If someone tells me he or she has committed murder, my sympathetic listening does not intend to encourage murder, but to encourage the telling of it. Thus I may not agree with the things I hear, and yet this has to be no obstacle to my genuine and open listening. Judgment of the person shuts off communication.

Speaking and listening are complementary arts, and as we are called to exercise now one, now the other, we can profit by our experience in one role to improve our performance in the other. To listen as we want to be listened to when we talk, and to speak as we appreciate the other person to speak when we listen. Our liking or disliking the other person shows immediately in our spontaneous though guarded reactions. Let us watch them to know ourselves better. We are not listening properly because we do not like the speaker. We are not inclined to speak because we do not appreciate the listener. We are free to choose our audience and to decide to whom we lend our ear, but once we do it, it is up to us to give ourselves fully to the occasion as befits sensible and responsible human beings. To do things by halves does us no honor and brings us no profit.

In general it can be said that a speaker gets the audience he or she deserves. If on the one hand I make up my mind to speak, but on the other I hold myself back, I hide facts, I disguise events and tell only half-truths, I cannot expect my audience to warm up to me and to be a model of empathy, acceptance, and encouragement. I am not giving myself up to them with total openness and sincere frankness, and they sense it and pay me back in the same coin with partial understanding and half-hearted applause. If, on the contrary, I open my heart with delicacy and sensitivity, but without dissembling or misgivings, I will soon see other hearts opening and other smiles widening before my open smile. People are quick to notice and generous to react. Genuine communication is a joy to both parts, and if the chance is offered, every alert person will wake up to it with zest and gratitude. If we do not often get such welcome reaction from people, it will be time for us to examine what it is in our attitude that keeps people back, that is, what it is that we are keeping back from people. If people pay no attention to me, this may simply mean that I am saying nothing.

Lack of contact in communication comes from fear, from expectations, from selfish preoccupations with one's own interests, from prejudice, from interpretation, from boredom at the length of the paragraphs, or from anxiety about the reaction expected. If dialogue is not satisfactory, this is a valuable hint for me to look into my own performance, both as a speaker and as a listener, and to discover the obstacles I throw into the process. "Tell me how you communicate, and I will tell you who you are" is a valid saying that prompts introspection, as I realize that to improve my dialogue is to improve myself. To become a good partner in dialogue is to grow as a person. Encounter is the school of character.

Here is an example of an old and fruitful relationship. The great *rishi* Vyas was resting after completing single-handedly, according to tradition, the writing of the main traditional Hindu scriptures, when the sage Narad, lovable busybody in all affairs of gods and humans alike, approached him and said, "You have written wise and holy volumes, but if you forgive me for saying this, nobody understands them. Only Brahmans read them and use them in their studies and prayers, but the majority of devout men and women are left without a scripture they could use. You will do a great service to humanity if you now write a popular scripture where all your doctrine will be exposed, but in such a clear and interesting way that all will read and all will profit from it. Am I not right?" He certainly was, and Vyas was also aware of it and ready to undertake the new venture. He had, however, one difficulty. He was older now, and his hand got tired when writing. He needed a scribe. Narad, a man of many connections, had soon the answer. Ganesh, the god with the elephant head, versed in many arts, indefatigable and obliging, would be ready to do the job. Vyas would dictate, and Ganesh would write down the text without ever committing a mistake. The dictation would continue uninterrupted, as neither the bard's inspiration nor the scribe's energy would ever fail; but Vyas then established a condition. He insisted that Ganesh would never write down a verse without first understanding it fully. That was no problem for Ganesh's intelligence, and he readily agreed. Then, on his part, he postulated another condition. He would stop only when his pen would lose its point and he had to replace it.

With that understanding, the work began and went ahead without a hitch. But then, each one had his own tricks. When Vyas wanted time out to plan a new passage, he would throw in a tough verse, so that Ganesh had to pause for a while till he could understand it fully, and that gave Vyas enough time to compose the verses ahead. And when Ganesh's hand got tired, he pretended that the pen was blunt, and took his time to change it and to rest his hand. Thus the inspired sage and the divine scribe got on famously together, the work went on with all speed, and the devout faithful, and indeed the whole of literary humankind, got a new masterpiece to last for all ages. That was the *Mahabharata*. Great poems come from the cooperation between a great speaker and a great listener who never writes down a line without understanding it fully. And a sharp pen to do justice to the noble thought. Mankind is grateful to Vyas and Ganesh.

Pack Your Own Luggage

"How can I reveal myself to you when I do not know myself?" This query brings us deeper into the understanding and practice of relationships, and uncovers the fundamental root of hesitation and shyness that keeps us back in our sincere effort to learn how to relate to others more spontaneously and effectively. How can I speak of self-revelation when I am a riddle unto myself? How can I show my true face to others when I am still to discover it myself? The greatest sages on earth in all climates and cultures have declared that the main endeavor of the human person is to answer the question "Who am I?" A whole lifetime goes in beginning to figure out the meaning of the question, let alone trying to answer it. And without its answer, how can I embark upon the communication that precisely depends on it?

We need a "face" for communication and friendship and life. No portrait will do, however skillful. It must be my own face, known, cherished, and possessed by me first, so that I can show it as my heart prompts me to do. And here comes the crisis. I do not know my own face. I do not know my soul, my character, myself. I have taken myself for granted, I have moved along with the general notion of my position in my family, in my profession, in my society. But I do not truly know myself. I do not possess myself; how can I now give myself to you? I am not in contact with myself; how can I enter into contact with you? I am dazed, beclouded, confused; how can I speak out my soul to you?

A beginning could be made by admitting that I am confused. That is a first and valid communication. It states things as they are, is candid and humble, and it prompts the almost inevitable answer that the other person is also quite confused about his or her own self. We are at least in the same boat. One of my professors in my long student years was a stammerer. It was painful to listen to his halting explanations, but we put up with them, given that he was a good teacher and we were good people. One day, in the initial rounds to know the students at the beginning of the course, he asked one of the new students, "What-t-t-t is th-th-the d-d-derivative of the co-co-co-cosine?" The student stood up dutifully and answered in a mocking mimicry, "Th-th-the d-d-derivative of the co-co-cosine is m-m-minus s-s-s-sine." We were all horrified and held our breath in anticipation of the impending storm. The professor, who was a kind character, had nevertheless been hurt, and said feelingly, stammering all the more for the repressed anger, "D-d-do not l-l-laugh at m-m-e; it is b-b-bad e-e-enough t-t-to b-b-be a st-st-stammerer." To which the student, pointing repeatedly at his own breast with eager sincerity, answered desperately: "I, t-t-too, am a st-st-stammerer!!!" Needless to say, that student was not asked any more questions for the rest of the year. (Today, for the consolation of all stammerers, he holds an important job in his profession.)

We are all stammerers in our lesson. It is good to know it so as to lose fear and enter more easily into dialogue. But if we are going to keep on stammering all the way, communication will become painful and the lines will be jammed with staccato consonants all over. It is time to untie our tongues, which means to untie our souls, solve our complexes, remove the veils and uncover our faces before ourselves so that we can then reveal them to others. In fact, one of the great benefits of this exercise in self-revelation is that it prompts us, directs us, urges us, to know ourselves in the first instance, and keeps on impressing on us the need and the way to advance in the all-important science of self-knowledge. There are ways to cure stammering if we are really serious in wanting to correct our faulty communication.

One step deeper now. We do not know ourselves because we have not made ourselves what we at present are. We are not our own makers in views, mentality, and outlook. We are largely the result of other people's convictions, practices, and influence. We have been shaped by family, atmosphere, and circumstances before we could shape ourselves by our own hand. This is, at the same time, an unwelcome indictment that hurts our pride and excites our protests, and a valuable hint to find the root of our impasse and get working at it. We have not made ourselves on the inside, in the sense that we have not chosen our surroundings, our heritage, our schooling, or our society, and we have been given from early childhood values and principles and habits and points of view that are quite noble and valuable in themselves but that we have not chosen by ourselves. Our mental makeup has been put together by other hands, loving, to be sure, and competent in their caring dedication, but outside hands after all, hands of parents and teachers and leaders and preachers who have molded our minds while we played unconcernedly the games of childhood and youth. By the time we woke up, our mental directions in life had been determined, and we found ourselves thinking, approving, disliking, praising, and rejecting the things we had been taught to think, approve, dislike, praise, and reject. This was convenient, perhaps necessary, and in any case, universal practice. We could move ahead on the roads of life with detailed maps and marked directions. This makes the journey easier, and so we tend to forget the preset nature of our trip. Among many things that are very fine in this arrangement, and for which we are grateful, it may also be good to be reminded that we have not packed our own luggage.

Nowadays this is considered dangerous; in fact, not to do one's own packing is a serious offense in modern travel, as I found by myself not very long ago. I was starting on an air trip, and as I approached the check-in counter, two hefty officers in the airline's uniform blocked my way and stated politely that they had a few questions to ask me. One of them pointed to the baggage trolley I was pushing along and asked me, "Have you packed your own luggage yourself?" I answered that such was the case. Then the other questioner, in what seemed to be a well-rehearsed sequence, urged me with a knowing smile, "Hasn't your wife helped you with the packing?" I meekly explained that I was a priest, and present Vatican regulations prevented me from obtaining the kind of help they seemed to be pointing at. My candid profession did not discourage them, however, and they wanted to know further whether I had left my luggage unattended for any length of time, which again I am not in the habit of doing, as I value my few possessions and would be loath to part with them for the benefit of any quick-witted professional on the premises. Had I then packed "any sharp object, any electronic gadget, any matches, lighter, or explosive substance?" By then I was beginning to think that it would have been quicker if they had opened my bags and had searched through them, but the procedure had to be followed and the questions answered. I passed the test, but was left curious as to what fate awaits the traveler who confesses that his wife has packed his bags for him. I feel proud of myself as I consider myself something of a packing expert, and I now realize I owe that blessing to my celibate state.

I do not want to go through life with luggage someone else has packed for me. However well-meaning and wise and kind that person or set of persons may be, I want to pack my own belongings and be personally responsible for what I carry along in my mind and in my heart. This does not mean that I am going to throw my bags out the window, but simply that I am going to open them in the privacy of my room and the peace of my mind; I am going to take out, one by one, all the items in them, have a good look at each, and decide, without prejudice or animosity, but out of my own will and personal decision, whether I want it now in my luggage, or rather want it replaced by some other piece of mental outfit in the cupboards of my mind. As simple as that and as healthy as that. And then I shall be able to answer for my bags and give all details about my own belongings. No bombs in my luggage.

I Love Myself, I . . .

One step is leading to another. The inkling that relationships shape us is proving true, as a little reflection on relationships has shown us how they require true communication; communication, in turn, is based on self-revelation; and self-revelation, of course, cannot take place without self-knowledge. Thus the living practice of close relationships makes us enter into a school of character that is going to train our minds and our hearts in the daily discipline of thought and affection. Any avenue that leads to self-knowledge is a royal road to growing fulfillment.

Self-knowledge does not come easy. I want to know myself in order to reveal myself to my friends, but when I try to undertake the task, I find myself blocked by hidden fears and blind reluctance. I visited the famed Tree-Tops Hotel in Kenya, and watched from the safety of the wooden gallery, literally built on the tops of the trees, the countless animals that came at night to slake their thirst in the large pond of water at the feet of our trees.

The guide explained to us that wild animals preferred to drink at night, because with daylight they saw their own reflection in the water when going to drink, and were frightened by it. We seem to have something in common with the animals of the forest. We bounce away from our own image.

If we do not look at ourselves, this is because we do not quite like ourselves, and this can be an important link with the idea that has started us on our considerations, that is, the realization that all affective connections in our life are double-edged, and love and hate alternate regularly in the vital cycles of our complex existence. If this is so with respect to others, it will also be with respect to ourselves, and we are faced with the interesting and not altogether unexpected fact that even for ourselves, we, too, are targets of hatred as well as of love. I love myself, and I hate myself. Indeed it could not be otherwise if we consider that our ways of dealing with others are fundamentally a projection of the way we deal with ourselves. We adopt an ambivalent love-hate attitude toward others, because in our own hearts we have adopted a similar attitude toward ourselves. Mixed feelings rule our life both on the outside and on the inside, and the study of our relationships is leading us to understand better the riddle we ourselves are.

It is not rare for people to dislike, more or less openly, some part of their physical or mental makeup. Once a girl who was talking with me in a roundabout way about her difficulties in social life suddenly broke down, began to cry, and painfully gave out the real cause of her sufferings and her complexes. "I don't like my chin," she said between sobs and tears, in a tone that precluded consolation. I tried to get a look at her from the side as unobtrusively as I could, and she was right. She couldn't very well like her chin, because she hadn't any. Her description of the situation was correct, but there was nothing I could do about her chin; neither could she afford plastic surgery to correct her façade. She would have to live with her chin, or lack of it in her case, for the rest of her life.

I have seen a bald man make outrageous jokes at his own bald spot in a desperate attempt to convince his listeners and himself that he took his baldness sportingly, while in truth he hated it and resented it from the depth of his being and had never reconciled himself to it, as his uncalled-for jokes testified. I have watched a young man who, by wearing long-sleeved shirts with closed collars in the sultriest days of the Indian monsoon, tried unsuccessfully to hide the white patches caused in his dark tan by that lack of pigmentation called leukoderma. Though harmless in itself and not contagious, this condition becomes hateful and socially unacceptable due to its popular name of "white leprosy," and to the unsightly contrast in the colors of the skin.

I have known girls who suffer from a stunted growth, or who hide for days while a stubborn conjunctivitis disfigures their eyes. And I have shared in the repeated agony of the boy or girl who, while alert and accomplished in many ways, fails to reach the official standards of academic institutions, and is obliged to repeat an examination or a whole year, with public disgrace and private suffering. Mental or physical shortcomings can be a cause of acute distress to the person they inwardly or outwardly deface, and none of us is entirely free from such failings. This makes it important for us to find and adopt the attitudes that can minimize the harm our defects can cause us.

We are exhorted to accept ourselves as we are, and there is all to be said for this healthy piece of advice, but this is more easily said than done. "Accept your chin as it is" might be the right textbook formula from a professional counselor, but I have no heart to tell that to the girl in front of me, while she is weeping and lamenting her facial appearance. It is obvious that she hates her chin, and the best line of approach, with tact and sensitivity, may be for me to help her say so without qualms or hesitation. In fact, she has said already that she dislikes her chin, and if I now say very gently and with love in my voice, "You really hate your chin, don't you?" she is sure to say yes with her head while her tears run down her cheeks. Let the tears run; let the ill feeling come out; let the hatred surface and find full expression in gesture and word.

The girl with the receding chin hates her chin, the bald man hates his bald spot, the leukoderma patient hates the white patches on his skin, and the failed students hate their lack of brains or memory or nerve to achieve what their peers have so easily obtained. Nothing is gained by minimizing the feeling and waving away the hurt. It is there, and its recognition is the first step toward its cure. I hate myself in this particular feature of my character or my physique, and I shall be lying if I say otherwise. Let me feel my anger and express my frustration. Only then can I begin to see how to right things inside me.

We have seen that our relationship with others begins to yield its secrets and improve in performance the moment we realize it is a love-hate relationship; and if that is true of our relationship with others, it is also true in our own relationship with ourselves. We, too, stand before ourselves in a double-faced attitude. We love ourselves, as we undoubtedly do in our own interest and out of our very first self-preservation instinct; and at the same time, in diverse aspects and in diverse ways, we also hate ourselves, as our experience amply shows and our memory testifies. And there is nothing wrong with it. On the contrary, we may have already experienced how our relationships with others improve when we know and accept the fact that they have always been, and will continue to be, love-hate relationships. And the same will happen when we turn the focus on ourselves and apply to the legitimate love we bear ourselves the analysis that examines all loves and directs them for deeper understanding and firmer practice.

This will carry on the self-acceptance principle to a further application and greater effectiveness. There is no question of accepting what we very well know we do not accept, or of saying we like what we continue to dislike from the bottom of our hearts; but we can accept the fact that we do not accept those traits in us, if this does not appear too much of a riddle for a start. It may look like hairsplitting, but it is simpler than it looks. The girl cannot very well say, "I accept my chin," because she does not, and no advice, counseling, or browbeating can make her say such a thing with truth and therefore with profit; but she might conceivably be led to say gently and tentatively, "I accept the fact that I don't accept my chin." That is, I accept the fact that I don't fully accept myself, I accept the fact that I dislike some things in myself, I accept the fact that I even hate myself at times. This can be more within reach for a start.

Take the case when I have been fairly defeated at a game. I can say that I don't mind at all, that the important thing is not to win but to participate, that I feel quite happy as the result was fair and my opponent played better; and if I say that, I shall be telling a lie, because that is not how I feel at all. Someone has said that there are two kinds of losers: the good losers, and those who do not dissemble. I have felt defeat, I feel bad about it, and precisely because the game has been fair and I cannot claim injustice nor even bad luck, I regret it all the more, I feel displeased with myself, and so in a small, passing, uneventful but real way, I hate myself for having played badly and having lost when I know I could have won with a little more effort and skill. So I feel bad, and I let myself feel that way. I accept the fact that my defeat has affected me, that I am not a "good loser," and that my feelings are going to rankle within me for a while. I need not say this aloud, and can show the outward smile while I congratulate my opponent on his or her victory, but I am clear about it in my mind, and that makes for inner peace and balance in the situation.

Again, to accept my hurting feelings does not mean that I am going to feel anger or frustration or pity for myself, but simply that I know I am hurt, I feel it, I do not hide it from myself, I take it as part of life in its checkered course, and I remind myself that the end of the world is not yet at hand. I accept the fact that I am no exalted saint, indifferent to pain and joy, if there ever was any, just as I am no professional yogi, indifferent to heat or cold, if there ever was any. I feel the changes in temperature, both in my body and in my soul, and I take them as part of the ups and downs of life without making any fuss about it or trying to fathom the ultimate mystery of suffering on earth. I have just been defeated in a friendly game, and that is all. I will definitely keep on playing.

Harder than dealing with physical defects or temporary setbacks is dealing with the stupid blunders we at times commit and the wrong decisions we unaccountably make. I do something that on obvious reflection after the event, when the decision cannot be changed anymore, shows to have been as neat a piece of idiocy as a feebleminded donkey could have perpetrated in a moment of weakness. And then I truly and deliberately put myself down and hate myself. How can I have done that? How can I have been so blind? How is it that I didn't see what inevitably was coming upon me once I did that? What will people say? And, worse than that, what can I think of myself, how can I trust myself, what guarantee can I now have that I shall not commit such a blunder again? How can I face life when I know myself to be such a fool? I hate myself for what I have done and for having undermined my own self-esteem and damaged my self-image. These personal consequences of the blunder are far worse than whatever incon-

venience it may have caused directly through the outside effects
of the misguided step. Self-hatred, however hidden and passing,
can cause havoc in our lives.

Early this year I was faced with one such decision, and I made
one such blunder. I was in India, busy with my regular work for
the year, when I received a rather unexpected letter from my
mother in Spain. She wrote that she felt her strength ebbing
away, she knew she could not now live long, she missed my help
and prayed to God for my coming. True, she did not force my
hand, but she was ninety-seven, she had had a sudden collapse a
few months before in my presence when the doctor told me that
could well be the end, or, at any rate, the beginning of the end,
and I knew her helplessness and my own desire to do for her in
her last days what I had not been able to do in all my life. I had
left her to become a Jesuit when I was fifteen, and came over to
India when I was twenty-four, without ever being able to repay
her for the admirable and abnegated way in which she brought
me up single-handedly after I lost my father at ten, and we lost
our home and all belongings in the ensuing Spanish Civil War.

I was not needed just then in India, as I have already retired
from regular teaching, and I could well go to my mother's side
and comfort her in the last stage of her life. What made my
decision difficult was that at precisely that time there was a meeting in India I was very keen to attend. A group of religious friends
were going to meet for fifteen days to collate spiritual experiences, evaluate memories, and dream together, and I had been
looking forward to that meeting for months. It was a unique
occasion, and it would not be easily repeated, at least for some
time. I would either make it or miss it. By then I was uneasy,
almost fidgety, argued with myself that the fourth commandment
took preference over my own personal interests, and cabled my
mother that I was coming.

I went to Spain, and found that the urgency was not so great. I could well have attended the meeting and gone to Spain afterward. The fourth commandment could have waited a few days, and I could have obtained both aims, the meeting and the visit, with perfect ease. But now it was too late. I had missed my chance. And I blamed myself with bitter vehemence and lonely frustration. I had spoiled my own interests with my own hand. I had rushed irresponsibly into the wrong conclusions. I had been blind, hasty, and thoughtless. I had not been in touch with myself, with my true feelings and my real needs. I had not sized up the situation objectively, had not weighed properly the circumstances, had not been balanced, cool, or serene. And I had bungled the issue. I knew all the theory of making right choices, I have given talks and written books about it, I have advised numberless people in their discernments and their decisions, and now that I come to make a simple decision myself, I go flat on it and make a perfect mess of it. I hated myself for it with relentless self-condemnation. The kind understanding of my friends, with whom I discussed my plight, only served to emphasize my discomfiture. I had blundered, and I felt miserable for my fall. By then I had come to realize that my pain at having blundered was now greater than my regret at having missed the meeting.

I tried to comfort myself with the words of Fritz Perls, which I had used to reassure others in similar circumstances: "Friend, be proud of your mistakes; for in them you have given out bits of yourself." It is true that in my mistakes I am very much myself, as I come through uncensored, untutored, unguarded. My mistakes are Freudian windows to my unconscious, and any chance to see myself as I am, and even, with some more courage, to show myself as I am, should be welcome opportunity for growth and contact. But transparent theories become fuzzy and muddy when one tries to apply them to oneself. I also tried to console myself with the confidential advice of a good neighbor and wise thinker, Bakul Tripathi, who, on the eve of my departure, had encouraged me with his personal experience of a persistent guilt complex for not having done for his parents all that, after they were gone, he thought he could have done. His open admission had been, for a moment, reassuring comfort to my troubled spirit, but when faced with the actual trial, I again felt alone and mistaken. Whatever the future would be, for the present I was desolate and depressed. The thought even occurred to me that this painful experience of mine could help me later in helping others, and indeed is serving me just now as a good illustration of an important point I want to make. But, honestly speaking, I do not enjoy the prospect of putting myself through inconveniences just in order to be able to tell others how it feels when one is under the weather. No, I could not find consolation in books or friends, and I just kept watching my own affliction with hurtful wonder. Only the candid admission of my error and the soothing passage of time brought slow healing to the gaping wound.

I need not belabor the point here to emphasize how this very incident brought home to me, in understanding and feeling, the reality of love-hate relationships with those who are closest and dearest to us, without anybody's fault but with everybody's strain. It will be plain, at least, that I am not writing on this topic out of books, but out of my own live experience and personal reflection. No better school of life than life itself.

Settle Your Bills

A situation largely responsible for the "hate" part in the love-hate relationship is the one just mentioned in the last chapter. I am referring to the always well meant and seldom well understood readiness of a person to sacrifice his or her own interests on behalf of another person held in special affection and esteem. This generous attitude of self-sacrifice can be made a measure of friendship between friends and of closeness between relatives. If I am ready to sacrifice myself for you, that means I love you, and my love for you is sincere; whereas if I recoil before sacrifice, stick to my interests, and refuse to bear inconvenience for another's sake, then my love is not genuine, and I am only selfish. Sacrifice is the test of love, and if I want to be a true lover, I must prepare myself for self-immolation in small and big things for the sake of those I love.

All this is very true, and can be very deep and beautiful, and humankind's history would be all the poorer if the pages where true sacrifices and genuine generosity have been recorded were torn away from it. Men and women can reach their sublimest heights when they come out of themselves in open self-giving with small, thoughtful attentions or total service unto death for their fellow human beings. But there is a snag to self-sacrifice, and it is important to uncover it and keep it within sight. Sacrifice implies a victim, and if the abnegated volunteer acquires a victim complex, this may harm the action, the process, and the persons involved. While a noble deed may have been performed, the secret feelings around it may be twisted and deformed, and prove detrimental in the end to both the subject and the object of the sacrifice. I do something for you today in what outwardly looks, and inwardly feels, to be a genuine gesture of selfless altruism, but I take note of it in the hidden archives of my subconscious mind, and claim later full compensation in open appreciation from you to me or in repressed resentment from me to you, thus hurting in any case our mutual relationship.

Bills are eventually charged in this world, and favors are never free. When the account is due, the reminder comes infallibly, and reminders of payments are never welcome. We may have thought that when we did something for another, we were doing it out of pure love and true concern without any mixture of self-interest; but our mind knows otherwise, and the outward service may well have carried a hidden hook to draw later advantages in justified compensation. Sometimes the hook shows, and any alert person, including the angler, may notice it; and sometimes it passes unnoticed, and does all the greater harm when it hits raw flesh. Here is a case where the hook shows, as told by Erik Blumenthal:

> The whole family is seated at the table. Sixteen-year-old
> Celia and her mother are serving the food and helping the

two younger brothers. Celia's father is carving the meat, and he pointedly gives the best slices to his wife and daughter, explaining as he does so how self-sacrificing he is. He grumbles about the children's table manners, then magnanimously offers around what is left of the salad before taking more himself. Then he calculates what a similar meal might have cost in a restaurant. Celia, of course, sees straight through her father's behavior, and certainly doesn't respond with the reward he is asking for—her appreciation. Her father rewards himself by demonstrating his generosity. If he had offered his family the best of the meal out of love, then perhaps he would be appreciated, but it would have been much better to have served it to them in such a way that the others had scarcely noticed him doing it. In that case the good he did would stay with him, meaning that he would become more positive, and would be in a better position to do more good. *

Here the father was naive enough to publicize his generosity, and got the deserved cold shoulder of the rest of his family. If you are doing something for us, at least have the elementary decency and social elegance not to rub our noses in it. And if you do, you have charged your bill and the transaction is over. More subtle is the case when the father feels clearly within himself that he is sacrificing himself to let his family have the daintiest tidbits in the meal, but he does not let his feelings show. There he is not charging for his service openly, but he does expect payment by way of affection and appreciation, and will be disappointed if it is not forthcoming. And the most dangerous case is when he does expect payment but is not aware of it and believes he has favored his family out of sincere and selfless love for them. Then the bill will be pending, both in his mind and in its payment, and the unsettled account will secretly erode the affection and confidence

---

* Erik Blumenthal, *To Understand and Be Understood* (London: Oneworld Publications, 1987), p. 96.

existing between debtors and creditor. Outstanding bills should be settled soon.

In India we have a very practical custom at weddings. During the solemn reception in which the bride and bridegroom stand in all their youthful charm and glowing elegance under the glint and color of an ornate canopy, the guests approach one by one in a disciplined flow of well-mannered disorder, greet and congratulate the happy couple, have their photograph taken with them for the album, and politely withdraw, leaving in their hands as they do so a parcel, a box, or just an envelope. The newlyweds gracefully acknowledge the offerings and quickly pass them on to someone by their side who, attentive and efficient, unobtrusively takes care of the incoming gift parcels and makes them disappear from sight into a secure hiding place. The invitation card for the wedding may have exhibited the printed rubric "No gifts will be accepted," but that is rather a reminder to bring the gift, and in no case an objection to its being promptly and gratefully accepted.

Before the gift is whisked off into safety, however, an important formality has to be gone through. A well-dressed individual is sitting by the side of the wedding throne with paper and pen in his hand, and he takes down the name of each donor together with the amount of the gift, if it is money, or its description if it is anything else. This carefully made and carefully kept list has an obvious purpose. When a wedding later takes place in any of the families that graced the wedding today, the list will be taken out and consulted, and the size of the gift to be brought to their reception will be easily calculated by referring to the gift they brought to the couple today, and simply matching it. Just a matter of practical arithmetic. As inflation can have been high in the intervening time, the price figure may be judiciously multiplied by a carefully calculated coefficient to make provision for

the inflation, and the gift will be chosen accordingly. This sim-
plifies matters. We know that the value of the gift will be properly
noted, and good relations between the two families will be en-
sured. A practical procedure to be sure. Debts are paid and accounts are settled in the joyful setting of a happy wedding. And
the lesson is learned not to leave people under an obligation, or
place ourselves under their obligation. Clear accounts help clear
relationships.

Mullah Naseruddin once reached a strange country where nobody knew him. But the people were kind and offered him all
kinds of help to settle among them. The tailor made clothes for
him free, the shoemaker offered him shoes to his exact measure,
someone took him to a house, some other gave him a job, and he
even obtained a wife and lived happily in the land. He was full
of praise for the hospitality he had found there, and often expressed his admiration for it to his wife. One day, when he
needed a new pair of shoes, he went to the same shoemaker who
had presented him with the first pair, and he made new shoes for
him, but this time he did request payment, charging double the
usual price. The same thing happened with the tailor when he
needed a new suit of clothes, and indeed with all those who so
generously had helped him in the first days. All charged double
for new goods, or asked for some other favor in money or in kind.
The mullah commented on this strange behavior of the people to
his wife, and she explained to him: "In our land, favors are paid
for. We are kind and patient, but we have a memory and keep
accounts. If we were to give free supplies to all those who come
here, we could not survive. But then, don't complain, because
they have also given you something for which they ask nothing in
return, and that is me." Naseruddin's chivalry prevented him
from contradicting his wife, but his sharpness prevented him
from keeping quiet, and he said: "Yes, but now they will ask me

to give them children in return." He always had to have the last word.

All this does not mean that we cannot do favors for others, that we cannot be genuinely of service to others, or cannot or should not sacrifice ourselves for them. What it does mean is that we have to straighten our approach to such acts of service, clarify our views and cleanse our feelings in the matter. It is not a question of the acts we do but of our inner attitude in doing them, and it is there that a little touching up may be needed in our ideas and in our practice. I will attempt to make this clear by means of an example.

The wife proposes to the husband that they spend a month abroad together, as both have free time and it is already long since their last trip. The husband sees the point and promises to think about it and give an answer, but from the first, he does not at all feel like a trip. He was counting on that month to do some work that needed to be done at home, he wanted the peace and tranquillity of a continuous stretch with himself and his wife in the quietness of their home, and the last thing he wanted for a vacation at this stage was a trip abroad. He knows all this very well, feels within himself the opposition to his wife's proposal from the start, is also conscious of his wife's desire to travel and of his own genuine inclination to please her whenever possible, and sits down to reflect on the conflicting wishes, and on the answer he has to give and the way to word it. A delicate exercise in domestic diplomacy.

He can choose to say no, and do so either bluntly or politely, with thoughtful compensations for the negative in other plans and in deepened affection, or with gruff definiteness in dictatorial terms. He does not want to go, and puts his foot down from the beginning without a chance for negotiation or a ray of hope. The matter is closed, and there will not be any trip abroad this year.

But he may also come to say yes, and this is the situation that needs some careful analysis if we want to understand the subtle play of reasonings and feelings in their hidden depths and their outward consequences. The husband now has two fundamentally different ways of saying yes. I call them, for clarity, "the victim way" and "the partner way," and this is how they work.

In the victim way, the husband thinks as follows, and the way he thinks will then, of course, determine the way he talks and the impression he causes, whatever words he may use to disguise feelings and hide reality: "I do not want to go, but just to please her, I'll go. I know that I always have to yield in the end, so I might as well do it from the beginning. No use putting up a fight when I know who is going to win in the end. I hate the very idea of a trip abroad at this juncture, and I anticipate a pretty horrid month in lousy surroundings and dreadful company. But I'll resign myself and sacrifice myself for my wife's sake as I have done so many times since the day we married. And let people see what an accommodating husband I am." Here it is clear that the husband does not want to go, yields only to please his wife, and feels and says and proclaims he is sacrificing himself for her in doing so. Whatever words he uses to announce his acceptance to his wife, his resentment will show through, and will grow and thrive through the whole month of unhappy vacation and the rest of his married life. In this case a considerate and reasoned refusal to go might have been better for the couple than the reluctant and begrudging acceptance. Clean dealings help common life.

The partner way takes quite a different approach, though the end result may appear the same. In it the husband thinks more or less along the following lines: "I dislike the idea of going out for our vacation, and I know it quite clearly. Still, all things considered, I decide that I want to go because I judge that in the long run this will be better for both of us. If I refuse to go, she'll get cross with me, is likely to get into one of her depressions, will suffer the whole month at home, and will make me suffer in the bargain. And even after that, there will be no end of recriminations and accusations and regrets for the lost holiday. On a purely selfish count, I get off more cheaply by going abroad, and so it is in my own interest to go. And if I go with good grace, she will appreciate it and will be nice to me in the many beautiful ways she can be when she wants. So I go, and I want to go, and will let her know so without delay." Here the logic is different. The husband is no fool, knows his own likings, and is perfectly aware that he does not want to go and, if left to himself, would not move from his home in the whole month. But he sees himself in the wider context of his marriage and his family; he realizes that his own good is inseparably linked with the good of those around him, and is sensible and bighearted enough to see that by making others happy, within the limits of genuine self-protection and legitimate personal aspirations, which in this case were certainly safeguarded, he himself will on the whole be happier. And so he goes willingly, and that makes all the difference.

The difference is not merely grammatical. Between saying, "I don't want to go, but sacrifice myself for her sake" and saying, "I dislike the idea of going, but judge that in the circumstances, it is better to go, and so I want to go for the sake of both of us," there is the difference that tilts the love-hate balance to one side or the other. If anything goes seriously wrong during the month abroad, the "victim" husband will find his chance and explode with ill-contained fury, "There you have it! *You* wanted to come, *you* have got us into this mess, and *you* now will please find out how we get out of it!" Whereas the "partner" husband will by then have integrated his decision into his life, and will be able to say with truth and understanding, "We both are in this together. Both of us wanted to come, and both together will now find the way out of this mess." It is easy to see which couple will have a better holiday.

It is perfectly possible and profoundly healthy to be able to say of all that we do in life, "I do it because I want to do it." No outside imposition, no foreign duty, no helplessness, no complying, no compromise, no disguise, no subservience. All that I do is because I truly and personally want to do it. Many of those things I dislike, I think mistaken, I disapprove of, I even regret. But in the wider and larger and deeper context of life and society and circumstances and authorities and history and future and heaven and earth, I calmly see that the painful option may after all be the less harmful for all concerned, and so I knowingly and willingly embrace it. This is one of the most liberating attitudes in life. Even in jail I will not be a prisoner, because, however unfair the sentence and cruel the guards and mean the fare, I will want to obey its rules so long as I am in it. It is the opposition in me to a person, a circumstance, an order, a trial, independent of the objective fairness or unfairness of the situation, that creates in me the bad feeling, the resentment, the violence, the hatred. Once I untie the knot of my inner opposition by truly wanting to do what I am doing, the atmosphere is cleared, pressure is eased, and I breathe contentedly. To incline our love-hate relationships toward their love end, an important step is to cease to be, or to consider ourselves, victims.

The Risk of Confrontation

To be effective in their fundamental role of shaping our lives, our relationships have to be well defined, strong, and sharp. A mild, distant, diplomatic attitude toward those we regularly deal with at home and at work may keep official peace conditions in a troubled world, but will not give us the strength, the solidity, the edge, that an individual person can and must have for impact and for growth. We need the chisel to carve the image. We need confrontation to fashion character.

Without a challenge, the person lapses into mediocrity. The great temptation of the least effort. Let be. Don't stir. Follow the crowd. Avoid trouble. That is the way many people live, by necessity or by choice, and those who want to go that way have a right to do so without being disturbed. But there is a price to be paid in conformism and laziness, and that is a lowering of the standards of being alive. The more I withdraw into myself, the less of a person I am. The flowering of the personality needs the wild air, the rain and the wind, needs the direct encounter with other persons to bring out the true self. No man or woman ever grew to greatness alone.

Therapy groups today have been called "encounter groups" in a spontaneous emphasis on the healing and growth-promoting qualities of the human encounter. Just meeting other people in the common arena of seeing faces, hearing comments, and speaking freely opens up possibilities, unveils vistas, and encourages action. And even outside controlled groups, the daily meeting with other persons, when it becomes a true meeting between human beings instead of a formal ceremony between rigged-up puppets, can be a school of self-knowledge and improved behavior. Far from shunning the daily encounters that freely offer us the training ground for our own advantage, we will do well to welcome them and use them with skill and gratitude to refine our presence in society for the good of all. The confrontation, when properly faced, does good at least to two people, and eventually to many. It is worthwhile entering into it.

Mullah Naseruddin once traveled to a land where he saw cock-fights for the first time. He was impressed to see the way the fighting cocks used their natural spurs as a swift weapon of deadly attack. Back in his own country, he took two freshly laid eggs and placed them on a table in front of each other to see whether they would fight. As a long time passed, however, and the two eggs showed no inclination to enter a personal contest, the mullah declared: "Now I know. The cocks fight only to sharpen their spurs."

The eggs, of course, have nothing to sharpen, and therefore nothing to gain from a mutual encounter. They would only break their shells and spill out their insides. They are still in the hatching stage and cannot be exposed to outside shocks. Let the live chicken emerge and find its shape and grow its talons, and it will need the fighting spells to find the assertion of its pointed personality. This is not to defend cockfights, if they still exist, but to profit from ancient wisdom and enjoy the seemingly naive wit of the Sufi masters. It must have taken quite a mock seriousness to watch patiently two eggs and see whether they would fight. Round shapes only roll.

It takes courage to confront another. I begin to feel that I want to bring up a matter with a friend. Something has happened that makes me feel uneasy, and I want a clarification to straighten up matters. At first it seems evident that something is wrong, and an explicit heart-to-heart talk is needed. Then I begin to doubt. Is the matter really true, or maybe it is only my own suspicion and I shall make a fool of myself if I mention it? No, it is definitely true; I am quite sure about it. Fine, but is it so important? Does it really have to be brought up, or could it simply solve itself by waiting and watching? Yes, possibly. No, definitely. When to speak up, then? Wait for the right moment. Days pass and the right moment never comes. I suspect that I am not so certain about the matter, and that is what makes me doubt and delay. I have turned the matter around so much in my head that now I definitely have to talk it out, if not for my friend's sake, at least for my own peace of mind and satisfaction. And so I finally take the plunge.

I choose a quiet moment when no one is likely to interrupt, and begin with what is intended as a nonchalant approach, but is in fact a stiff introduction: "I say, I . . . I want to speak about something to you if you don't mind." I notice that my voice has changed as I speak. I feel awkward and formal. I sense how my friend has at once taken notice and has stiffened imperceptibly. "Yes . . . ?" The air between us could be sliced with a knife. The phrases I had so carefully rehearsed look silly now, and I say something, correct it at once, then correct the correction, then smile, then frown, then blurt out whatever was on my mind in words that I know do absolutely no justice to the situation nor to my feelings, and wait for his reaction without daring to look at his face. He has listened with a patent strain, and when I finish, he says, "I have absolutely no idea what you are talking about. I have not experienced any estrangement between us these days; my feelings for you have not changed at all, and I cannot figure out what has made you talk the way you have talked."

So I put my foot into it. I got the signals mixed up, and saw red where the color was rosy. There was nothing the matter with him, while there was something definitely the matter with me, which had made me grow suspicious where there were no grounds for suspicion. Even so, it may be worthwhile now to talk this matter out with my friend, that is, my groundless suspicion, as that now seems to need clearing up, and in any case, we may turn out with a regular confrontation in our hands. And who knows? Maybe in the end it will appear that he *had* in fact noticed something, but was not ready for a showdown and had tried to evade the issue at the start. Given our mutual goodwill and mutual good feelings, the issue will be helpful for our relationship, but not without some strained expressions and awkward moments.

There is risk and there is pain in confrontation, and that is what makes it valuable. I may go wrong in my appraisal, and my partner may go wrong in his or her reaction. I do not know what I am going to get. In fact, the word "reaction," though very much in use now, particularly in this kind of confrontation, is itself misleading. A reaction is always conditioned by a preceding action, and this conditioning may limit its scope and preset its direction. Thus the reaction may become self-defense, and since the best defense is the attack, it may in turn become an attack against me, and the confrontation may degenerate into a regular duel between both of us, to the distress of both. The word "response" in this case is better than "reaction." We listen with interest, may even be aware that we also listen with apprehension, and we feel free to say so and clear the air through candid admission. Then we let our feelings surface, own them, express them, and wait for a further response. Then the dialogue has a better chance.

Common mistakes in confrontation are to attribute motives, to interpret actions, to denounce hidden schemes, to express condemnation. It is always rash to attribute motives to someone, when even that person may not be able to discern honestly what his or her own motives were in acting that way. It is very hurtful to hear someone tell us, even with the best intention in the world, "I know why you did that. It shows through even if you don't admit it. Anybody can see it." We ourselves are not sure why we did it, and here is this person who seems to know with decisive certainty why we acted the way we did. This is unfair and irritating. It will take a lot of sincerity and patience to respond properly, without flaring into anger and without withdrawing into spiteful resentment. Feelings are likely to be excited in a confrontation, and this, while dangerous, can prove very helpful, because feelings are, after all, the very warp and woof of relationships, and whatever straightens out the feelings, enhances the fabric.

A vital element in a confrontation is discerning the motive that moves us to risk it. Here is where sincerity and clarity and profundity will be required for a thorough searching of our own mind before we embark on the adventure. My motive in confronting my friend must not be to improve him or her in ideas or in behavior, and if the motive is such, my communication is condemned to failure before it starts. I am not out to improve anybody, and I want to purify totally my interaction with others, and especially any confrontation I may start, from any trace of patronizing zeal that, under cover of wanting only their good, may try to tell them what they should do, avoid, correct, or take up. Such an attitude ruins communication. Even my own personal improvement, taken separately and exclusively, is not the proper motive for a confrontation. That would be using my brother or sister for my own profit. The proper aim of a fruitful encounter between two persons is the improvement of the relationship between both. I care for him or her, care for myself, and know that this relationship can benefit both of us and is at present passing through a crisis, which I can solve if I express it and we meet together and thrash it out. This attitude will open channels and make contact. And with real contact, we can expect that all concerned will profit.

When a country is attacked, all citizens unite together, factions disappear, and a new and strong unity is felt over the land. A similar effect can take place when a person is confronted by another in emotional exchange. A confrontation is, however well meant and properly carried out, an attack on a person as a person, and so an immediate effect of it will be a rallying together of all the dispersed facets of the individual in a concerted effort to face the situation. We are often scattered abroad in dreams, imaginations, fantasies, skirmishes, smoke screens, avoidance tactics. Our strength dwindles because our resources are spread out. Now, a practical way to call back our troops and unite their command is to enter into confrontation with a healthy outlook and serene approach. The trumpet call sounds in our mind, and soon all our attention, our wits, our determination, our willpower, our courage, and our faith spring to action and combine forces in a holy crusade. A well-conducted encounter always has this positive effect of restoring inner unity to both parties. And when both parties are strengthened, their mutual relationship also profits from their newly acquired strength.

There is also the possibility that the confrontation may backfire and both parties may be hurt, and their relationship may be badly shaken. Even then it was worthwhile to take the risk. If the relationship is broken by the frank talk, maybe it was not so strong after all, and if it was going to break up later, it is better that it does so now. And in all likelihood, even if there is now a temporary estrangement, if the relationship was genuine, it will reassert itself, and the two friends will come together again with deeper feeling and greater confidence. Confrontation helps to undo prejudices, to know oneself better, to appreciate one's friend, and to value the friendship. Real confrontation is based on trust in oneself and in one's friend, and on the desire to deepen the relationship by all means within reach, and to purify it from possible doubts and reservations. At the end, one finds that there was nothing seriously wrong, and life goes back to normal with a smile of relief.

Mullah Naseruddin once saw a group of policemen in the village square, and immediately turned to run away from them at full speed. The policemen chased him with equal zeal through street after street and into the open fields around the village. Suddenly Naseruddin stopped in his tracks, turned around, and faced the police. The policemen almost fell on him with the impact, and finally stopped also and surrounded him. When all had regained their breath, the mullah asked, "Why did you chase me?" They answered, "Because you were running away from us." "Well," countered the mullah, "now I am not running away from you." To which the head policeman answered, "Neither are we now chasing you." And thus the confrontation ended. This is the story of many a misunderstanding between friends.

The Lighter Side of Things

To be vulnerable is not to be weak. On the contrary, only a strong and mature person can afford to know his or her own vulnerability, to accept it and to let it be known. A weak person will hide his or her weakness, will avoid struggles and put up defenses for protection and flight. A heavy armor always hides a weak character.

How do I enjoy a joke at my expense? Do I feel threatened, uneasy, unhappy? Do I smile awkwardly to hide an embarrassment I do not want to be known because it would betray an annoyance I am not supposed to feel? Do I cut the general amusement with a frown, censure the joke, and change the subject forcibly? Or do I truly enjoy the dig someone has given me, laugh freely and wholeheartedly, join spontaneously in the general merriment, and congratulate the joker? If I am not ready to be brushed even by the gentle stroke of an innocent joke, I may well begin to examine why I am so hypersensitive, so suspicious, and so insecure. Outside overprotection is a sign of inward weakness.

During my mathematical studies I had the opportunity to observe different kinds of teachers. The greatest among them was a bit of a genius in the field, extremely knowledgeable, widely informed, bright in his approaches, and charmingly hopeless in his elementary mistakes with simple calculations. He was open to any suggestion, would change halfway the long proof of a theorem at the slightest provocation, did not consider it below his dignity to ask for our help when he got stuck with a new problem, and willingly admitted that he had been mistaken in an answer and would try again the next day to come up with the right one. He knew his subject and much more than his subject, and we knew that he knew, and he knew that we knew that he knew, which made it perfectly safe for him to plead ignorance instead of trying to cover up a slip with a violent tour de force. He was eminently vulnerable, and his great capability was precisely the secret of his disarming vulnerability.

On the other hand, halfway through the first year, a new teacher joined the staff, and we were his first students at university level. He was rather raw, unsure of himself, hesitant, and not entirely in command of his subject. He did not admit questions in class, forbade any interruption, and would run away as soon as the bell rang for the end of the period in order to avoid being accosted and asked questions in the corridor. He knew his weakness and protected it with a fortified front all around. He could not afford to open himself to questions or suggestions because he was afraid he would not have an answer. He never became a popular teacher. His favorite escape was "Come here next year, and I'll explain that to you," meaning that we were only beginners, and had to learn more and join the higher class in order to be able to understand his learned explanations. It was nothing of the kind, of course. We knew his bluff and smiled to one another knowingly. After some time nobody asked him any question or asked for any explanation from him. We knew it was useless, and would not waste our time. We simply wrote him off. The management wrote him off, too, at the end of the year.

Teachers who say, "Don't interrupt me!" "That's a silly question!" "I don't answer your question because you would not understand the answer," "If you had paid attention before, you wouldn't ask that now," and similar avoidance clichés are only proclaiming to the four winds that they are not ready for the questions, and, what is more serious, that they are not ready to accept the fact that they are not ready for the questions. To master the classroom subject or not is a purely academic matter to be considered and dealt with by the authorities of the institution; but to refuse to admit one's weak points and to try to cover them up is a much more serious matter that affects the person, and therefore the teaching, in a much more fundamental way. The teacher may teach correct mathematics by sticking to a painstakingly prepared lecture; but if he or she suffers from the avoidance complex due to personal insecurity, his or her teaching may cause harm in the students, who will subliminally learn the wrong attitude of closing up before others instead of candidly opening up and owning difficulties as they are really felt.

Vulnerable teachers are lovable teachers, and they can teach more by their ignorance than by their scholarship. Let the students learn that they can accept mistakes without shame, failures without embarrassment, and ignorance without disgrace. Let them learn from their teachers, not as a lesson for the examination, but as an example in real life, that they can win greater appreciation by manifesting their limitations than by hiding them. Let them watch their own feelings bend in recognition before the candid defenselessness of a sincere elder. Let them realize that an open house is a more inviting place than an impregnable fortress. Lessons of the classroom for life outside it.

The teacher's case is only an example. We all have our own ways of saying, "Don't ask such questions!" "Don't trouble me," "Don't get too close"; and the effect is the same as in the case of the teacher's injunctions. People around us see the armor and keep away. We feel unequal to the meeting because we do not master the subject. We are not sure what we want to do with our lives, and we are not doing it anyhow. But we do not need to master the subject in order to talk about it. In fact, a good way to open a conversation can be to admit that we are at a loss for some answers. This will set at ease all those around us who are as much at a loss for answers as we are, and true contact can be established. Vulnerability opens us to friendly relations with our fellow humans, since they are as vulnerable as we are. In weakness, once more, there is strength, and our salvation lies in understanding this truth and living up to it.

To be vulnerable means to show feelings; to admit that we are not indifferent to praise or scorn, to comfort or hardship, to success or failure; to reveal moods and confess to envy and anger and disappointment and anxiety. To be vulnerable means to recognize that we are not always happy, not always in the best of moods, not always masters of ourselves, not always sure of what we are doing. To be vulnerable means to be human.

Maybe the best compliment we can pay a person is to let our vulnerability appear before his or her sight. This is a gesture of courage and trust, is a true gift of ourselves to the person we want to befriend. We ask people who visit us to make themselves "at home," to be "at ease," to be "informal and relax." All these are expressions meant to make it easy for them to feel well and free with us. But those are only spoken words, which may have the opposite effect of making those visitors more self-conscious and stiff and formal. A more efficient way to put someone at ease, with due regard always to situation, circumstances, and interest we have in intimacy with the person, is to show unobtrusively and tactfully our own weak points, to relate a recent faux pas of ours or a joke on ourselves, to share a doubt or a perplexity. The door has been opened, and anybody can walk through it if so desired.

Part of the appeal of the stories and personality of Mullah Naseruddin comes from the fact that he appears as a poor fool who blunders his way through life, provoking laughter and sympathy from those who watch his amusing antics, and then leaving behind a gentle trail of hidden wisdom that enlightens and encourages without any burden or strain. In his learned introduction to a collection of 461 original Naseruddin stories, José Luis Vivas Bailo writes:

> In 1124 another oriental writer, Al Maydani, gives us some more data about Yehá [Naseruddin's title is given as Yehá, Hodja, or Mullah, according to where the story proceeds from]: He belonged to the Banu Fazara tribe, and his real name was Abu-l-Gusn. More important for us, apart from these details for the researcher, is the fact that he quotes an expression which even today is common currency in almost all areas of Arab-Islamic culture; that is "Ahmaq min Yuha" which means, "A greater fool than Yehá," and is commonly used and understood in all popular Arabic languages. *

He calls him an "antihero" who, through his naïveté, his laziness, and his inborn cowardice, eventually gets the best of every situation and defeats the schemes of the powerful with the simplicity of his foolishness. Thus to become "a greater fool than Yehá" is paradoxically to obtain the rare wisdom that makes us go

* José Luis Vivas Bailo, *Cuentos de Yehá* (Seville: Tomás García Figueras, 1989), p. 5.

through life with a light heart and a winning smile. Naseruddin had just that valuable quality.

One of the first stories of Naseruddin's childhood is the following. When he was a small boy, his mother had to go to a wedding, and she left the little Naseruddin alone at home with the injunction "Take good care of the house door while I am away." The boy sat down to watch the door, while the mother went to the wedding. After a while, Naseruddin's uncle came from a village, and on being informed by Naseruddin that his mother was not at home, he instructed the boy, "Tell your mother that I have come from the village, and that tonight I'll come to stay with you." And he left. Then the boy got up, took the door off its hinges, loaded it on his shoulders, and went to the place of the wedding to inform his mother of the uncle's arrival. His mother was surprised to see him carry the door bodily, but the boy explained, "You told me to take good care of the door, and Uncle told me to tell you he had come; so the only way to obey both of you was to do what I have done." The mother rushed back home, and found that robbers had entered the doorless house and had taken away everything. She bewailed her lot, and the uncle later joined in the lamentations. Meanwhile, the boy had got what he wanted: to attend the wedding! And we get the advice not to take things in life too literally.

And now one of the last stories on Naseruddin's death. He had gone walking to a far-off village, where he was given the news that he had died. He was rather surprised at the news, but as everybody in that village seemed to be talking about it, he finally believed the news and lay down on the ground as if dead. The people gathered around him, and he told them, "I am dead, so please go to my village and inform my wife that she may prepare my funeral." Some people turned to go, but the mullah stopped them and said, "Maybe she will not believe you if you tell her, because she saw me this morning quite strong and healthy. I'd rather go myself and inform her personally about my death; then she'll certainly believe me." The people countered, "What you say is right, but you are now dead, so how can you walk back home?" The mullah saw their point, and after some thinking, found a solution: "True, I cannot go by myself, as I am dead, but you can take me there." The people put him on a stretcher and carried him back to his home. There he gave his wife the sad news of his own death; she started weeping and beating her breast and told all to depart and leave her alone with her grief. When she was alone with her late husband, the mullah, who was still dutifully lying down on the stretcher, she quietly told him, "So you finally got what you wanted, didn't you? A free ride back home!" There was at least someone who could see through the madman's madness. And blessed be the fool who can fool around this way with the idea of his own death.

Riding a Donkey

Mullah Naseruddin is traditionally represented riding a donkey backward. The donkey is, of course, the poor man's mount, the simpleton's companion in toil and in joy. The position of the rider, facing the donkey's tail, makes the picture funny in any case, and poses the question of the reason for that eccentricity. Only the mullah himself could give the true answer, and, in fact, he gave several, as though to suggest that his apparently clumsy actions were too full of meaning to be exhausted by a single explanation. Once he said that his donkey was left-handed, and that was why, in deference to it, he mounted it from the other side and ended up facing the rear. On another occasion, when his disciples were following him, he explained to them from his back-to-front throne that that was the proper way for him to ride, as only then could he do justice to his own standing and to his considerateness for others: As their master, he had to ride in front of them, and as a polite man, he did not want to ride with his back to them, and he had found the perfect answer to the problem, as he always did. He gave still a third explanation, but I do not consider it to be in sufficient good taste to print here. In any case, his definitive answer is the one that has to do with the donkey's own nature as understood by humans. The donkey always does the opposite of what it is told, and so the mullah explained how, by sitting with his face toward the rear, he made the donkey believe he wanted to go in that direction, which was enough to make it go in the opposite direction, that is, forward, as he secretly wanted to do. There was no lack of ingenuity, in any case, to explain an outlandish gesture.

When we, humans, attribute different behavioral traits to different animals, we are simply projecting on them our own peculiarities. If we say that donkeys are thickheaded and stubborn, we are only recognizing that we ourselves are thickheaded and stubborn on more occasions than we care to number, and with a contumacy that defies description. We enjoy doing the opposite of what we are told or requested or expected to do, and sticking to our position, with total disregard for its objective justification or lack of it, against public opinion and private advice, and for unreasonably long, extended, open-ended, and sometimes never-concluded periods of time. Donkeys would not have endeared themselves to us as they have done if we had not recognized in them some of the most precious qualities of our own character.

In the love-hate game we are engaged in throughout our lives, we all have periods of obstinacy in which judgment is blinded, senses are dulled, reason is suspended from its functions, and we stick unaccountably to an attitude, a belief, or a posture out of a sense of misunderstood dignity and hardened pride that can endanger the best of relationships and cause pain to ourselves and to others in an unnecessary estrangement. Feelings are ruffled, harsh words are spoken, looks are averted, and physical distance

is allowed to mark with its observable effects the mutual alien-
ation of two people meant to live close together. Spells of silence,
staccato monosyllables, knit eyebrows, minimal contacts, and
prolonged absences. No yielding, no compromising, no taking
the initiative to break the impasse. And hours may pass and days
may pass and the rift may continue under the dogged inflexibility
of two people who love each other but do not want at the moment to act accordingly.

The trouble with such alienating periods is that during the
affective separation, the mind grows wild, the resentment in-
creases, unpleasant memories are exaggerated, and aggressive fantasies are indulged in, with the result that the image of the other
person is greatly distorted, unpleasant features are enlarged, and
reconciliation becomes harder. When we love a person, we see
him or her in a glowing light; positive qualities are enhanced and
negative ones diminished, and this improved perception in turn
helps our feelings and strengthens our bond. In just the same
way, when we feel temporarily estranged from that same person,
the light changes; the positive qualities all but disappear while the
negative ones are emphasized in our mind to the distortion and
disfigurement of the original image. These changes in the image
greatly influence our later behavior toward the person whose
image that is. This makes it important to watch our own mind in
its unpredictable vagaries as painter of images.

Hector Berlioz's *Symphonie Fantastique* is a musical example
of what a change in feelings can do to change an image, this time
a musical image. The theme that runs through the five-
movement symphony is the "theme of the beloved," which describes in sound and rhythm the lovely figures and characters of
the most beautiful of women as seen by the most infatuated of
men. When the theme first appears, in the charm and innocence
of the first idealized love, it is a pure melody of haunting beauty

and lingering fascination. Each note follows the previous one in an increasing cascade of transparent sound that leaves the soul with the firm artistic conviction that there is nothing in the world, nor can it ever be more beautiful than the supreme perfection of the beloved one. But the love is not returned, and as love turns to hatred in the rejected lover, the music turns to dissonance, and the certainty to doubt. The theme now appears disconnected, interrupted, torn, and the same notes that first expressed beauty now depict uneasiness, torture, and despair.

But the worst is still to come. In his desolation, the artist dreams he has murdered the beloved one, is accused, convicted, taken to the scaffold, and executed among the wails of the orchestra in agonizing chords. His soul descends into hell for a Witches' Sabbath of unspeakable horror. And there, in the midst of the witches' screams and the devils' curses, and to the dismal accompaniment of a hideous parody of the *Dies Irae*, the motif of the beloved appears again, but this time so distorted, so mauled, so twisted out of shape and sound and sense, that it brings distress to the soul and anguish to the spirit in a mad whirlwind of broken notes.

When another great composer, Felix Mendelssohn Bartholdy, heard the symphony for the first time, he pronounced it "utterly loathsome and unspeakably dreadful," and declared that after listening to it, he had not been able to work for two days. Such is the effect produced by the raw contrast of a heartrending theme pronounced first in love and then in hatred. The theme is the same, as indeed the lover and the beloved are the same, but something has changed in the heart of both, and the change is expressed in the ruthless music which rends the soul apart with the very strength of its discordant blows.

Beauty can change to hideousness as love turns to hatred, and the change is fostered by the misunderstanding, the distance, and the silence. The irony of the case is that when Berlioz wrote his symphony and explained its meaning, he had not yet met the object of his love, the Irish actress Harriet Smithson, who at the time did not even know Berlioz. It was all a play of the artist's wild imagination, as indeed most infatuations and quarrels are. When contact is lost, or when it did not even exist from the start, thoughts run riot and build up extravagant fantasies which support one another in an irresponsible spiral of increasing spite and final rejection. Stubborn isolation leads to grief, in music and in life.

In India the custom still obtains for the bride, who, on marrying her husband, has gone to live with him at his parents' home, to go back to her own parents' place when the time comes for her first delivery, or indeed on some other occasion, and stay there for a period before coming back to her husband. Normally the going and coming takes place without a hitch, and after a reasonable while the husband, on a previously negotiated date, goes to fetch his wife at her parents' house and comes back with her. That is the standard procedure. But sometimes hurdles may come in the way. If any friction, unpleasantness, or conflict occurs, a feeling of rejection may be felt at the start. If this feeling is fed by wild thoughts divorced from reality at the distance, physical and mental, of a different home during several days or even weeks, the result can be a refusal to come together again. Friends and families can also take part on both sides, so that in the end, a private quarrel becomes a social confrontation. Then both parties stand on dignity, and the same argument is heard on both sides. The husband says, "She went on her own, and she can come back on her own when she wants; but I am not going to fetch her or call her back." The wife echoes, "It is his duty to come and fetch me back, and I'll go willingly with him; but I'm not going on my own." The perfect stalemate. You are welcome to come back, but I'm not coming to fetch you. You are welcome to fetch me whenever you want, but I'm not coming if you don't come first. By then, both people in their heart of hearts are longing to put an end to the disgraceful episode and come together again and live in peace; but neither will take the first step. How long the deadlock will last is anybody's guess, and indeed everybody's gossip in the social circles of both the families.

In such occasions I have sometimes taken the liberty of suggesting a simple procedure. I request that a map be brought forward, and the place of the two homes be marked on it clearly. Then, by purely geometrical methods, the midpoint of the segment joining those two places is to be found, and the astrologer to be unavoidably consulted for an auspicious moment. At that very moment and in that very spot the husband and the wife are to appear simultaneously from opposite directions, and the meeting is to take place to everybody's satisfaction. Nobody wins and nobody loses. Which means that everybody wins, and the impossible situation created by a mutual and irreconcilable stubbornness comes to a happy end. Unfortunately my method has not found wide acceptance, and headstrong people continue to give trouble to each other and to those who care for them. Geometry does not seem to work easily in practical life.

Mullah Naseruddin used to give his donkey its fodder every day, but one day he felt lazy and asked his wife instead, "Go and give the donkey its fodder." The wife was not pleased with the order, and they started to argue about who should do the work. As they could not reach an understanding, the mullah finally said, "Let us agree to this: We are going to keep silence, and whoever speaks first will feed the donkey." The wife agreed, and both shut their mouths with firm determination.

Naseruddin went to a corner of the room and sat down there in obstinate silence. His wife soon got bored, and she went out to their neighbors' house, where she remained the whole day till sunset. She told them what had happened and added, "He is so stubborn that he is ready to starve to death before yielding before me. Let us send him hot soup, since he'll be hungry by now." They gave a pot with boiling soup to the boy of the house with the order to give it to Naseruddin.

Meanwhile a thief had entered into Naseruddin's house and had begun to take all that he could lay his hands on. When he saw the mullah sitting motionless in the corner, he thought he was a paralytic, and he boldly took even the cap the mullah was wearing on his head; but the mullah did not stir and did not utter a word.

He was in that same position and attitude when the boy with the soup came. The boy said, "I am bringing you this soup from your neighbors' house." The mullah tried to make him understand through signs what had happened, how a thief had come and had taken away everything, even his own cap. To signify the loss of the cap with the turban around it, he pointed to his own head and circled it several times with his hand. The boy understood that he wanted the soup to be poured on his head, and proceeded to do so, unmindful of the temperature of the liquid. The mullah received the hot, sticky shower on his head, but did not move and did not speak. His face and his beard were badly disfigured, and the boy, on seeing his pitiful state, went back at once to report on all he had seen and understood; the theft, the soup bath, and the mullah's silence.

The wife realized the situation and went home at once. There she saw her husband, exactly in the same place in which he was when she had left, absolutely motionless, weeping and smiling at the same time, and she asked excitedly, "What is the meaning of all this?" The mullah answered, "Go and feed the donkey, and don't be so stubborn anymore."

The donkey got its food at last.

The Awesome Mixture

A tennis world champion declared to the press that he played best when he hated his opponent. In fact, he gave that as a partial explanation of his defeat in an important game: He had lost the game, he said, because he was playing against a friend, and he had not been able to bring himself to hate him on the court. That had weakened his drive and softened his touch, and the final result had gone against him for lack of aggressiveness in his game. The reasoning did not, apparently, apply to his friend, who had won easily while keeping his friendly feelings. Still, when I heard that, I felt a black shadow saddening my heart. Sports are fine, and championships are necessary to encourage them, but if a player has to nurse hatred in his or her heart in order to obtain a trophy, the time may have come for us to reconsider the shape we want our sports to take.

In fact, sports in their origin, as Greek tragedy or public recitals of epic war poems, were meant in part to "purge" feelings, to channel instincts of violence and aggressivity into harmless fantasies, and thus to avoid their being carried out in fights and bloodshed. The Greeks knew the dark side of the human heart, feared its promptings, and strived to neutralize their effects. Aristotle had given them the word "catharsis," which we still use, and their best poets and sportsmen helped to purify the people and the nation from the evils of unrestrained violence. The Greeks did fight, like any other people, but it is to their credit that the Greek Olympics never became the Roman Circus.

A grimmer example was given by a terrorist who, when asked to kidnap a rich but otherwise kind and pleasant family man, had to steel himself to hate him, as he later confessed, through thoughts and conversation with his fellow kidnappers, in order to gather strength for the brutal abduction. As he observed his victim before the attack day after day, and saw him play with his children, kiss his wife, and greet kindly all the people he met, he felt he could not inflict the cruel blow on the kindly man. He forced himself to think against him, to imagine his crimes, to talk about him as an enemy, so that he could finally pounce upon him, blindfold him, and carry him away. Hatred had to be brought into play to carry out the dastardly deed.

Sad realities of life on earth. There is power in hatred, and violent men and women know how to whip it up in the hearts of individuals or in the crowds of entire nations to make possible hostile actions that no person in sober sense would even think of committing. The cobra, we say in India, has to be excited that it may strike.

The warning for us is that what the statesman, the terrorist, and the sportsman are doing on purpose with full consciousness, we may be doing inadvertently, to our own harm and that of those we live with and care for. Living together always brings friction, clashes, resentment, opposition; while in the open we soon make up and smile again and renew friendship, down within us we may carry out a hate campaign in wild thoughts, black fantasies, and murderous desires which we by no means plan to put into practice, but which in their own dark and efficient way may predispose us for anger and conflict in unexpected ways. Thoughts breed action, and repressed unkind thoughts may lead to open unkind actions.

If I bring up here these depressing considerations, it is precisely because there is also a bright side to them. If there is darkness in the midst of light, there is also light in the midst of darkness, and if hatred can be fostered in the midst of love, love also can be fostered in the midst of hatred. If there is despair within hope, there is also hope in the midst of despair, and this simple fact can open for us a way out of inward crises and somber moods. This is the way to defeat defeatist beliefs and find hope and strength for action when we feel discouraged and despondent.

It is painful to list the negative things we tell ourselves in the privacy of our self-talk, but it is important at the same time to reveal our secret files in order to thwart the silent offensive that can be our undoing. A sample: "Nothing can be done," "Things can only get worse," "He (she) will never change," "We have gone too far, and now there is no undoing the damage," "Keep on the mask, hide feelings, and carry on the farce; there is no other way," "If I try to improve things, they'll get worse," "I am at the end of my rope," "I am beginning to understand why people can think of suicide." The tape can go on and on, and its deadly music can carve out grooves of despair in the matrix of the soul. Thoughts against ourselves, against life, against others who represent around us the inimical situation in which we feel trapped. Potential seeds of personal troubles in our social life.

And here comes the bright side I am alluding to. As hatred breeds in a love situation, so love can breed among thoughts of rejection. Each one of the phrases just mentioned, and each one of the situations they represent, also has its opening of hope in the contrary effort, as true as there is blue sky between dark clouds, and flowers on thistles. It is not true that nothing can be done, that things can only get worse, that we have reached the end, that humankind is evil, and we are without hope. There are true feelings in the worst of us, and ways out in the most oppressive circumstances. We are a mixture, and if that has made us search for evil in our humble goodness, it will also prompt us to search for goodness in ourselves and in others when life deals roughly with us and we sink to believe that all is lost and we are helpless and humankind is upon us for our perdition. Scrutinize the mixture and find the redeeming trait. It never fails to appear if we only search with faith.

I am not particularly gifted as a counselor, but with a bit of common sense and a lot of patience, I have repeatedly seen husbands and wives, who had come separately to announce that that was the end and nothing could be done, heal a final rift, come around and soften up and see light and attempt once more what they had given up as radically impossible. "He is that way and I have tried enough and he'll never change and I cannot take it any longer." Pause. "Could you tell me something good about your husband?" Silence. "At least one good thing for a sample?" Pursed lips. "Not even if you try hard, very hard for once just to please me?" "Well, if you insist, yes, he does behave normally at times." "An example?" Finally the example comes, however tenuous, and once the tap is open, the current flows and good memories come and nice things can be told where before there was only darkness and rejection.

Then the eternal objection: "But he [or she] will never change." I know the textbook answer, but I also know that if I want to have a chance of easing the tension, I must not give it at once, or rather not give it myself at all, but let questioners find it out by themselves, letting them believe it was their own find and thus likely to work if they give it a try. What the textbooks say is that the declaration "He [or she] will not change" is likely to be a projection, that is, a subtle, disguised, and self-justifying way of saying, "I am not ready to change." This cannot be told to the victim straightaway, of course, but she (or he) can gently be led to realize that she is intelligent, generous, and considerate enough to initiate a change herself, and watch with interest whether this produces some change in her partner. Life is not simple, and this elementary tactic will not resolve all problems, but it is remarkable to see how many improvements can begin on such a homemade basis. And the principle behind it is the same: the mixture. If we found a dead branch in a flowering tree, we can also find a flower in a dry bush. And where there is a flower, there is a spring.

This is an awesome example, perhaps historical, and at any rate immortalized in beauty and stone, of the eternal mixture of the best and the worst in the hearts of humans and in the monuments of their history. The Taj Mahal in Agra is perhaps the most beautiful work of art in marble and stone extant today after centuries of civilization in all climates and cultures of the planet. The sudden surprise of its first appearance as a white recumbent profile through the distant outpost of the red gate that stands watch to protect the view and awe the unprepared visitor; the slow approaching pilgrimage between the long pool of low water and the silent lines of vertical shrubs; the growing perspective of the majestic image; the four white prayers that pierce the heavens as slender minarets; the exact dome of geometrical perfection; the immensity of the structure that dwarfs all visitors while the proportion of its measures makes it easy to encompass and enjoy in a single view of wonder and joy; the reverent covering of the shoes to tread softly on hallowed ground; the steely softness of the surging walls; the rainbow landscape of the inlaid filigree; the sacred mystery of the Quranic calligraphy; the shadow of human death; the presence of the tomb. Uncanny summary of life and death in words of silent stones.

Emperor Shah Jahan had it built in longing memory of his best-loved wife, Mumtaz-i-Mahal, who died in childbirth. He searched the country and the world for the best artisans, the best stones, the best jewels, that would give shape to his intimate dream, and above all, he used his knowledge and wisdom to engage the best architect who would mastermind the wonder of ages. Ustad Isad was the man, and he agreed to put his art at the service of the royal love. His first sketches, however, did not satisfy the exacting emperor. And then comes the story that tourist guides tell in muffled tones under the mute witness of the funereal vault. To make the architect share the depth of his own bereavement, the emperor had Ustad Isad's fiancée killed, and the personal grief of the saddened architect in the parallel loss inspired the eternity of the stately mausoleum. The architect worked for his lost love, while the emperor contemplated his own. And we are left speechless at the beauty of the monument and at the complexity of the human heart. Mixture of passions in the simplicity of a unique art.

A Bed for Four

One more attempt to unravel twisted strains in our complex hearts. I said previously that since there are many parts to our complete selves, we also need several friends to respond, between them, to our different needs. This is not a handicap but a blessing, as it enlarges our affective circle and allays the sense of insecurity that would ensue if we depended on a single person for our emotional welfare. Before drawing the consequences from this important fact, I reinforce the idea with a wise quotation from Lillian B. Rubin in her book *Just Friends*:

> Throughout our lives, then, we have friends and "just" friends, old friends and new friends, good friends and best friends—each relationship meeting some part of ourselves that cries out for expression. One friend taps our intellectual capacities more deeply than others, another connects most profoundly to our emotional side. One calls upon our nurturant, caretaking qualities, another permits our depen-

dency needs to surface. One friend touches our fun-loving side, another our more serious part. One friend is the sister we wish we had, another offers the mothering we missed. The depth of a friendship—how much it means to us, whether we say we're "friends" or "best friends"—depends, at least in part, upon how many parts of ourselves a friend sees, shares and validates. For what a friend sees and reflects back to us is at once important in affirming and validating the various parts of self as well as the whole gestalt we call a self. Speaking about the range of possible friendships, a fifty-three-year-old woman gave voice to the fantasy of a peerless friend with whom all parts could be shared: "At the ideal end of the spectrum would be the friend who knows and can value all parts of you. What I mean is, supposing you have ten parts to yourself. With most people you can interact and share maybe one or two of them. Sometimes you get lucky and you can share more than that. And once or twice in a whole lifetime maybe, with real luck, you find someone you can share all of your ten parts with. Then you only have to hope that, as any of those parts change in yourself, they'll continue to mesh with the other person. Or, if you're luckiest of all, you'll both keep changing and growing in the same direction. That's asking a lot, maybe too much, isn't it?"*

Beautiful words that lift the mind to a momentary glimpse of paradise on earth, and strengthen our step in the joyful search of the ideal friend. And serious words that make us reflect that since along the road we are going to meet and need several traveling companions, we'll do well to consider the situation beforehand and measure distances and foresee frictions that are bound to arise as we advance in our way and pass through broad meadows and narrow straits in the unpredictable pilgrimage that life on earth is. The sharp paradox is that we need more than one friend to avoid the anxiety of having only one string to our bow, and

* Lillian B. Rubin, *Just Friends* (New York: Harper & Row, 1986), p. 56.

that the very fact of having more than one friend may and will create conflict situations between them and, closer to home, anxiety again in our own hearts. Here again the love-hate polarity comes into force with all its demanding urgency. Important growth opportunity for us to consider and to profit by.

One of the most awkward situations in my life, which out of its very clumsiness turned out to be comic at least for me, occurred when two religious sisters, both good friends of mine, came to visit me in the same place and at the same time. Both lived outside my city, had come here for a one-day buying spree in the city's large markets, and when their shopping was over, both had thoughtfully taken time out for a brief visit to my place before they went back to their respective homes. So they coincided, almost simultaneously and unknown to each other, in the small, discreet parlor designed for austere visitors in my regular residence. We sat on three upright chairs, and I took care from the start to place my chair equidistantly from the two they occupied, as I know gestures are important and wanted to maintain the proper balance in a polite setting.

I had sensed a dark foreboding in the pit of my stomach when the two visitors had been announced, and was determined to do my best to save the meeting from being an outright washout. Fat chance did I have. At the very first greeting I realized that what I most needed to have with me at that moment was a stopwatch. I had to gauge finely to a split second the time I addressed each one of them, as any real or imagined lengthening of the time given to one showed immediately as a personal affront on the face of the other. As I spoke to one of them, the other stiffened in her seat and looked daggers at me, bidding for her time. And when I turned to the second, the first froze in annoyance as if to gather strength for her next innings. I tried looking at a point on the wall midway between the two and speaking at the same time about some neutral topic that would apply equally to both, but then both sulked. It even occurred to me to look at one and speak to the other and vice versa in a crisscross effort to maintain contact with both at the same time, but they were utterly confused by the maneuver, and so was I as I started mixing the references and misdirecting the smiles. They just did not speak beyond monosyllables.

I knew I had to end the meeting at the earliest juncture, and I also knew that I had to contrive for them to leave at the same time, because if one left and abandoned me to the other's wrath, my inborn chivalry would be put to an overly severe test, which I wanted by all means to avoid. In this they readily cooperated, as neither of the two was ready to leave me alone with the other, not even for a moment, and so when one of them consulted her watch, the other immediately checked her time, too, and both rose simultaneously, to my untold relief and eventual release. I saw them off at the gate, but did not tarry to watch their course upon the road. They fortunately had to go on different trains.

I am in no position to say that women are more jealous than men, and probably it is not so (men, too, can be utterly petty and miserably jealous), but in my long experience of cherished friendship, I have never found myself in a similar situation with my male friends. I often meet with more than one at a time, and the common presence enhances the communication and deepens the joy. This does not mean that I have never felt jealous with them. As I reflect, I realize this has happened particularly at the beginning of a new friendship. When a man begins to be someone special to me, when vernal feelings burgeon in the spring of the soul which knows nothing of age, when growing closeness is guessed with the glowing anticipation that kindles the long hours of daily toil and earthly weariness, when a new face enters my private album, a new name acquires hidden music, and a new birthday is remembered with joy, then, if I see that man engaged in cheerful conversation with another of his friends, I feel the pangs of envy gnaw at my heart. I know it is insecurity that makes me tremble secretly and irrationally in the delicate tissues of my fragile self-confidence. Am I safe with him? Is he safe with me? Where do I stand with him? Don't his younger friends mean much more to him than I can ever hope to mean? Is it only kindness and goodness on his part that prompt him to spend time with me, or is there a real feeling in his heart for me as there is in mine for him? How can I ever know? Or yes, I know, because feelings have faces, and love speaks, and friendship makes itself known without certificates; but my shaky possessiveness wants to make sure that I do not lose what is beginning to be precious to me.

That is the bright side of a dark feeling, the mixture again in the permanent conundrum of our conflicting emotions. Jealousy, in a twisted but genuine way, is a compliment to my friend, a proof that I value the relationship and treasure the friendship, a message to myself to do all that I can not to lose what is so valuable to me. If the humiliating feeling is uncovered before the friend in trust and openness, it can, in fact, cement the friendship and close the gap, if any existed.

Once I saw a very close friend of mine greet very warmly and effusively a friend of his after a short absence, and something snapped inside me. He has never greeted me with such effusiveness or made ever so much fuss about me even when we have met after longer absences. Where does that leave me? I have seen it with my own eyes. I am evidently down in his list, and my claims of a special place were mere illusion. Strange to say, and chastening to recognize, but a simple, innocent scene can undermine the strongest of relationships in the shortest of times. Fortunately for me and for my friendship, I had by then set up a clearinghouse for mutual feelings with my friend; that is, we had learned and agreed together to communicate with each other whatever we felt about ourselves, in particular whatever could endanger our relationship or cloud our friendship. Accordingly I sought the occasion, plucked up courage, and told him about what I had seen and heard, and my interpretation of it. He laughed wholeheartedly, and his loud and spontaneous laughter was more reassuring to me than any oath of eternal loyalty. He did not even bother to argue the point or give any explanation. But he said one beautiful thing. "Wait, Carlos," he said. "Let years pass and time speak, and both of us grow older and look at each other, and then you will tell me where you have stood with me and continue to stand, as I know I stand with you."

He was right, and he uncovered for me with his words and with his subsequent unfailing and unsurpassable friendship the secret cure and happy transformation of early and immature jealousy. Let time pass. Let years tell. Let feelings ripen and characters settle and common memories increase and trials be endured and joys shared, and then friendship blooms with the irrepressible strength of youth and age and experience and faith, and old fears are exorcised and doubts conquered and insecurities overcome. Mutual confidence in affection is the fruit of loving perseverance.

Close to jealousy in the light-and-shadow play of our mean- ingful relationships is the unhealthy though almost unavoidable practice of comparing friends and missing the good qualities of some by looking at the supposed higher virtues of others. As we have clearly established, we have to move and live among varied friends, and this situation may easily lead to our setting one against the other in private evaluation, with the danger of creat- ing within ourselves and with them tensions that could well have been avoided if we had dropped the measuring rod for a start. The theory was easily stated when I wrote that different friends satisfy different needs in us, and so together they can effectively cover the totality of our personal facets. But then those facets are not so clearly defined, and those friends not so sharply divided, as though we were a geometrical pattern with regular polygons fitting exact measurements in a ruler-and-compass construction.

The different aspects of our personality overlap, just as the characters of our friends do, and we cannot just place ten friends before ten aspects, each one to look exclusively after one portion without interfering at all with the others. Things do not work that way. So the several friends remain, and their multiple jurisdictions in our relationship mix and interact and enrich our life just as they complicate it. Here comes the delicate and delightful task of valuing each friend fully for what he or she is, giving all their rightful place in our lives, and giving ourselves to them without reserve and without boundaries. The dividing of our personality into plots to be entrusted to different neighbors for exclusive use was only a parable to shed light on the matter. In real truth we belong fully to each of our friends as they belong to us, and the giving of ourselves fully to each, emphasizing his or her unique contribution to our life while preserving the totality of our commitment to each, is the tantalizing and blissful essence of human friendship at its best.

A more dangerous threat of the blight of comparison between persons is when we tend to compare, not our own friends among themselves, but our friends with other people's friends, or, for married people, their partners with other people's partners. Yes, I have a wonderful husband or wife or friend, but look at that other lucky person's wife or husband or friend; are they not much brighter and cleverer and smarter than anybody around me? No wonder in social gatherings I have to take a backseat, as my own company does not come up to what others can boast of in glamour and wit. Why can't I attract to myself the dazzling characters other people seem to gather so easily around them?

That would be a deadly approach to human relations. It is obvious that some people have greater brains or better looks or livelier conversation than others, but what matters in the relationship is not the market value of the person (with apologies for the commercial term), but the personal bond. There are, of course, sterling qualities in each of my friends, but what binds me to them, what I value and prize and treasure and would give my life for, is not their brains or their looks or their wit, but what they have come to mean to me, and I to them, in affection and understanding and commitment and love. This is priceless and heavenly and unique. And this is above all comparison or evaluation or jealousy. I will not bargain a grain of real friendship for all the glamour in the world.

This puts an end to the legendary search for the ideal friend. There is no such thing on the map. There is no catalog with alphabetical entries for easy reference. There is no first and second and third. But there is the flow of life and the circumstances of existence and the succession of events and the play of chance and the casual encounter and the sudden kinship and the growing closeness and the molten unity and the lasting trust. This is the ideal in its only true shape, the long and patient workmanship and faith that find in human weakness the breath of the divine.

A man well past marriageable age (if there is such a thing) was asked by his friends why he had never married. He answered, "I've spent my life looking for the ideal wife." His friends commented, "And, of course, you did not find her." He protested, "No, no, I did find her at the end." "But then what happened?" inquired the curious friends. "Oh, nothing," he explained, "it just turned out that she was looking for the ideal husband." No way for a match.

Mullah Naseruddin lost his wife and decided to marry again. To keep the propriety of things, as was his wont, and ensure the right balance, he chose a widow for his second wife. They married, and went along peacefully sharing their mutual thoughts with open trust. His new wife had not forgotten her previous husband, and her favorite topic of conversation was the recital of the virtues and wonders and attentions of the man she had first married and who was now dead. Naseruddin on his part also thought of his late wife, and there was no end to the loving reminiscences and exalted praises he devoted to her memory.

Things went on that way in the mullah's home till one day, while he was in bed with his wife, he pushed her suddenly and she fell down from the bed and broke an arm. Her father, when informed of the mishap, came to inquire solicitously about his daughter, and asked for the facts. Naseruddin was ready with his explanation: "I will tell you exactly what has happened, and then you, as the just man you are, can see the truth by yourself. There were four persons staying together in this house of mine: my wife, her late husband, my late wife, and myself. I am a poor man, and my house is small, and so is my bed. It could not very well contain four persons, and so my wife, who sleeps at one end of the bed, turned carelessly in her sleep, fell off the bed, and broke her arm. That is all." The father-in-law understood. There is no bed big enough for four.

Waves at Play

I am walking in the open. Long strides, fast step, head high, and eyes open and alert to take in color and movement all around me, far and near. I am conscious of my breath, which links the inside of my body to the wide range of the earthly atmosphere which is life in my lungs and blue air in the unending sky. I feel my skin, which is both a boundary and a bond between me and the world around me. I tread gently on the earth to save it from the blows of my heels, and to save my bones from the hammering punishment of the hard soil. I let my arms sway in pendular accompaniment to the rhythms of pulsating life in dancing crops and bending trees. I claim my place in the orderly ranks of children of nature, and feel inside me the organic oneness with all that moves and breathes and just exists with me.

I sing as I walk. I sing aloud, unmindful of the wondering smiles of passersby, of a forgotten line which I fill in on my own, of a note out of place in the melody. I find myself singing songs of my childhood, long forgotten and suddenly reborn, that quicken my step as the cells in my tissues remember the youthful strains of earlier days and springier moods. *"Trarira, der Sommer, der ist da!" "Auf der Lüneburger Heide," "Alle Vögel sind schon da," "Ein Jäger aus Kurpfalz," "Steige hoch du rote Adler!"* I wonder how the old rhymes come to life, find their places, claim attention, strike their notes, and fill the air as a loud proclamation of unity in my life from the days in which I learned those songs to the days I sing them now, and I realize how sound and air and feeling and vibration restore unity to a fragmented nature in all its living parts. I sing my life as I walk the ways of unending surprise in labyrinthic joy.

I love nature, in the majesty of mountains and rivers, and in the simplicity of a forlorn flower or a fallen leaf; in the open spaces of unspoiled wilderness, or in the limited edition of a municipal garden; in static photographs or in living presence; in thrilling movies or in ecstatic contemplation. I can bow to the rising sun in the Vedic rite of *suryanamaskar*, I can see the course of human life in the waters of the Ganges, can fall on my praying knees on a mountain summit, and can feel one with the starry mystery of a dark night in silent revelation. I love nature with awe and gratitude, with closeness and distance, with pride and humility, with newness and eternity. Cosmic feeling of human depth in infinite dimensions.

And then I hate nature. The whimsical weather, the murderous typhoons, the treacherous tides, the sudden earthquakes. The smallness of humans before the elements, the inclemency of the seasons, the insecurity before never-known changes, the depths of the oceans where so much human life lies in watery graves. One never knows when lightning will strike or storms may bear down, when the air will revolt and the feared whirlwind will grab and spin and torture the sands of the desert and the lives of

men and women who had made it their home. Helplessness of
the small before the large, of the contingent before the permanent. Precarious condition of humans on earth.

And the heat, the heat, the heat. The one persistent curse of
my life upon earth, and, I hope, no future omen of punishments
beyond. The relentless oppression, the air on fire, the burning
sun, the withered twigs on withdrawn bushes, the silent birds
with their songs dried dead in their thirsty throats. After a walk on
willpower and perspiration for necessary exercise, I wipe my pulsating forehead with my own hand, and fine grains of white salt
garland my fingers. The sun had first drawn out, and then dried
on my skin, the salty sweat that converts my forehead into a
private salt factory. And, once in my room, the oozing walls, the
settling dust, the solid slice of molten lead I am called to breathe,
the compassionate ceiling fan that moves the heat around with a
wailing singsong that sounds like a well-memorized apology for
not being able to do more.

The night brings no respite from the day's ordeal. The bed
burns, the sheets stick, the air bears down on the body in its
merciless stillness. The clock far away strikes hours which always
seem too early to the restless mind. Darkness smolders between
two fires, never too far from one of them. The night between two
days. The previous conflagration that lingers in embers, and the
coming eruption that announces its flare-up in the glow of the
now inimical dawn. Day after day. Month after month. The
year's seasons melted into one steady flow of a perpetual tropical
summer, with the bare rest of a brief and shy winter. Strain on
the body that bears on the delicate meteorology of the climates of
the mind.

What has gone wrong with this lovely planet that we have to
defend ourselves against the elements, subdue nature, fight for
survival? We freeze with cold or burn with heat, we are drenched

in the rain or parched in the sunshine, we are threatened in welfare and existence by wind and water and fire. Could not the lands be so distributed on the globe that continents were kinder and climates fitter for human habitation? Could not ocean currents and seasonal winds be so directed as to temper the inclemencies of the weather and make it easier and pleasanter for humans to dwell on compulsory earth? Could not our earthly home be a little more of a home? Heartrending cries of climatic distress.

And now I am sick in a hospital bed. Nature again, this time not from without but through the inside plot of viruses and bacteria, has struck with deadly aim at the very entrails of my vulnerable being. Discomfort inside, apprehension and fear, weakened limbs and coated tongue, physical pain and mental agony. Nights without sleep and days without rest. When will the fever go? When will strength return? How can confidence be regained when the sudden onslaught issues no warning and my innocent senses detect no sign? I hate the sight of the ceiling, the weight of the bed sheets, the taste of hospital food, the knocks at the door when I was touching sleep, the sympathetic questions, the repeated advice, the compassionate platitudes. I hate it all and I hate them all, and I only want to get out of here and steady my feet and walk fast and far, ready to reach my tomb but never willing to surrender to sickness again. Why should I be so frail?

Love and hatred. Fear and hope. Far and near and inside me and all around me. One day I was swimming in the sea, favorite sport in the freshness of the water and the freedom of weightless movement under the primeval kinship with the element from which all life emerged in the dawn of creation. A slight movement turned the whole body, the friendly waves caressed my relaxed limbs, the crests and the troughs rocked me with the cradle songs they knew so well from practicing them on all beginnings of a new life. Carefree joy in the arms of loving nature. But then suddenly I panicked. I knew the enemy. I had forgotten time and tide, but I knew of the deadly undertow that struck unannounced and carried away from the shore and toward the deep sea in the iron grip of its hidden current whatever body would be floating in its domains. I tried to swim, but the more I swam toward the shore, the farther I was from it. I flayed the waves, I felt the water turn bitter in my mouth, I fought the current, I sensed despair. An alert lifeguard saw my plight, swam up to me tied to a rope, and towed me to safety. I had seen life and death in a day, and my heart had sunk in hatred after it had swum in love. Unfathomable nature like the playful and murderous waves of its infinite oceans.

Gossip for Eternity

In writing about nature, I have already written about God. It is a convenient cover to express indirectly regrets and complaints about life and creation without blaming God directly, since we are not addressing him, but effectively involving him as he is ultimately responsible for order in his domains. And so the main point of this book, which I clearly stated at the start and which has been in my mind always through the varied settings of the different chapters, comes now to be applied to the chief and most important relationship of our lives, our relationship with God. And that main point is that every relationship is a love-hate relationship, and that the understanding of this fact is the best way to foster the relationship, while the ignoring of it damages the relationship and thus causes harm. It will take delicacy and courage to apply this to our relationship with God, and this is the task of this chapter, made easier, I hope, by all those that have preceded it.

I love God. It is not only the first commandment, but the basis of my life as a believer and the continued experience that has given sense to my thought, and growth to my affection. The youthful love for the newly discovered Friend, the thrill of his voice in the Gospels and of his presence in the Eucharist, the sacramental identification in the seal of the priesthood, the mature years, the growing intimacy, the closer understanding, and then the mystery again and the worship and the surrender and the cloud of unknowing. And the long learning to extend that love to all people in his name, to serve and to help and to comfort and to cherish. Branches from one stem, flowers from one root, love from one source. All the best in life, which is love and friendship, and which I trust the pages of this book have made clear how much that means to me, comes from that supreme love in the remoteness of the divinity and the closeness of faith and sacrament. The golden thread that weaves life into one.

But then I also resent God. (I spare him the harsher word out of innate reverence and literary manners.) I resent him for having taken away my father when I was only ten, for having made me see war and death in tender years, for the pain and suffering he has brought to those I love most, for trials in my family and tears in the eyes of my friends; I resent him for having given me hopes he never fulfilled, for not listening to my prayers while he promised he would, for dryness in prayer and solitude in celibacy, for the tension to uphold his claims in a world that ignores them; I resent him for giving laws I cannot fulfill and commandments I cannot keep, for making me feel guilty and threatening me with displeasure and punishment, for straining my faith and abusing my goodwill; I resent him for allowing some of his representatives on earth to say and do things that, in my best and sincere understanding, go against his own interest among us, his eternal glory and the good of his Church, and for the anger and sorrow and frustration this situation brings to me in my burning desires and utter helplessness. Oh, I resent God more than anyone on earth, precisely because he matters most to me and because in a mysterious but real way he is in every thorn that wounds my feet and in every burden that bends my soul.

I feel better after writing all that, and this confirms the point I want to make all along. Negative feelings, if ignored, minimized, or repressed, do harm first of all to the relationship itself, and then to others onto whom they are unavoidably diverted in hidden compensation for the frustrated love; and on the contrary, if they are acknowledged, accepted, and properly expressed, they heal and deepen the relationship and they safeguard all other people in our love from the vicarious vengeance that threatened them. If I feel that God has let me down, but out of reverence or fear or routine do not allow myself to think that way and continue to tell God that he is wonderful, most kind, and infinitely just and loving in his mercy and providence, and that I love him and thank him and praise him all the more for his marvelous deeds, something has gone wrong along the line and I am definitely in for trouble.

The first trouble is that my words do not correspond to my real feelings, and this conscious or unconscious cheating is going to undermine the relationship and in the long run weaken my faith. Faith is strengthened by speaking up, not by keeping quiet. Grievances are grievances, whether true or imaginary, and they should be aired in time, with trust and clarity, or else they will deepen and fester and kill. And the second trouble is that if the poisonous tide of resentment has risen in my soul and I have blocked its way in the direction it had by itself taken, it will continue to rise, and, finding its first way blocked, will find other outlets and pour itself out onto other targets, to the surprise of innocent victims of my mislaid anger. If I do not clear up in time the misunderstandings, frictions, and clashes arising more or less openly in my relationship with God, soon all persons around me, and particularly those who work under me and are in consequence easier targets of my ruffled feelings, will find themselves attacked and maltreated in one way or another with unsuspected vehemence and without justifying reason. They are paying for the squaring of another account in which they have no part. The chain always breaks at its weakest link.

Job cursed the day in which he was born and the night in which it was said, "a man has been conceived." In his poetic language and in his unalloyed sorrow, he was clearly thinking of the Lord who made that day and ruled that night, and to him was addressed the savage cry of his wounded heart. His friends told him to shut up and confess his sins, but God appreciated more the sincere complaint of his devoted servant than the political appeasement of the diplomatic friends. He took up the challenge directly, spoke up with equal clarity and even greater vehemence, gave rise in his speech to some of the most sublime expressions of divine revelation, and eventually reinstated Job in his possessions and his happiness. Transparency in a relationship always works for the best for the people involved and for the relationship itself. And our most intimate and delicate relationship, which is our relationship with God, is not an exception but a clear confirmation of the rule.

I do not quite know, as the veil that protects divine faces from human gaze prevents crude rationalization, but it is just possible that at God's end of the relationship, his relationship with us, men and women on earth, may also be a love-hate affair. He did express some strong feelings against his own people in the years of the desert and the prophets; and today with us, as people and as individuals, he may also at times feel really fed up and harbor genuine grudges against us in the midst of his unfailing love.

This, however, is for him to say.

Gossip for eternity.